The White Tribes of Africa

by the same author

P. R.: The Fifth Estate

The Road to Number 10
(with Anthony Howard)

THE White Tribes of Africa

BY RICHARD WEST

Photographs by John Bulmer

THE MACMILLAN COMPANY, New York

First American edition, 1965

The Macmillan Company, New York

Library of Congress catalog card number: 65-21063

DESIGNED BY RONALD FARBER

Printed in the United States of America

Contents

Prologue

PEOPLE ARE shy of calling the whites whites and the blacks blacks. This is not so in most of Africa, where all races affect to wear their color with pride. Therefore few readers in Africa should take offense at a book about the whites in black Africa. But even if the phrase is not offensive it needs some clarification. The white people concerned are Europeans, people of European descent, like the South Africans and the Americans and, stretching a point, the Israelis. If I include Israelis and not Arabs, it should not be taken to mean that I deny the Jews their new home in the Near East. It is simply that they are mostly European in birth or heritage and that the Africans think of them as white people. What of the Asiatics in Africa? The South African Government, with characteristically hair-splitting pedantry, has ruled that the Chinese are colored but that the Japanese are white. South Africa has valuable trade links with Japan. But to include them in this study would too far extend the real theme, which is the role in black Africa of the white peoples who were or still are its rulers.

Now that the meaning of "white" has been defined here, it is still necessary to define black Africa. The phrase was once used to refer to the part along the west coast above the bulge, where the very dark-skinned Negro people lived. It can be and has been argued that the Bantu people of southern Africa—everywhere south of the bulge—are actually brown-skinned. It is an over-subtle distinction. Roughly speaking, black Africa can be defined as the continent south of the Sahara. Admittedly there are some black people living in or north of the Sahara, but only to the south are they the prevailing race. The countries of North Africa are outside the theme of the book for two reasons: they have been part of the Mediterranean, and therefore European world for several thousand years; and the natives and Arabs living there are fairly light-skinned. For both these reasons the presence of Europeans there have created less racial or cultural tension. This distinction between the areas north and south of the Sahara does not please the Pan-African parties, but it is well understood and appreciated by most whites, blacks and Arabs.

Considering that North Africa had been highly civilized since ancient times, the whites were slow to penetrate south of the Sahara. By the fourteenth century the Arabs had advanced down the east coast to Mozambique and into West Africa as far south as what is now Ghana. Even the Chinese had penetrated into black Africa by this time, and it is not right to laugh at them these days when they talk of historic friendship with Tanganyika or the Congo. Whether friendly or not, they certainly made contact, and a giraffe was taken to Peking zoo in the Middle Ages. At this time most European states were insufficiently stable or strong to venture on long exploration. What energies they had to spare went on the Crusades. It was not until the late Middle Ages that first the Venetians and then the Spanish and Portuguese went in for long-distance navigation. The Portuguese first explored black Africa. By the end of the fifteenth century they had sailed round the Cape of Good Hope and had opened a route to the Spice Islands and India. They were soon to be followed by the ships of Britain, France and the Netherlands.

These first explorers were not settlers. They built forts on the coast to act as supply stations for the voyage east, but only in the middle of the sixteenth century did they turn much attention to the economic exploitation of Africa itself. Then merchants followed the soldiers to open up trade negotiations with the African rulers of the interior. The names they gave these stretches of the shore speak for the nature of the commerce: the Gold Coast, the Ivory Coast and the Slave Coast. The spoliation of Africa had begun, and for centuries there was no evidence of a civilizing mission to compensate for the depredation. The whites often claim that they brought civilization to black Africa. But they did not begin to bring it until the end of the last century.

Until that time the whites had settled only at the extremities of the continent. The climate of North Africa is agreeable. The Europeans have always been eager to settle there—provided the Moors, Arabs and Turks have not objected. By the end of the seventeenth century the Dutch and a handful of English, Germans and French Huguenots had come to appreciate the temperate sunshine of the Cape. Between these two extremes there was no real white settlement. Malaria, yellow fever and other diseases made life vile for the Europeans in tropical Africa. Almost a third of all the newcomers to the coastal settlements died in the first year. Nor had more than a handful of Europeans ventured into the high, central plateau of the continent.

White penetration into the interior did not properly begin until the nineteenth century. It was encouraged by three things: Christian evangelism, the discovery of quinine as a cure for malaria, and power politics. Not all these explorers were men as saintly as David Livingstone. For instance, Stanley of the Congo, Speke of Lake Victoria and Burton of Lake Tanganyika—the brutal eccentric who translated *The Arabian Nights*—were all in their different ways egomaniacs. Britain likes to think that she settled Kenya only because she was trying to stamp out the Arab trade in slaves from Uganda. But Stanley, in the employ of King Leopold II of the Belgians, opened up the Congo to the far worse slavery of the rubber plantations. If Burton sometimes collected money for his trips by proposing to stamp out slavery, he did in fact approve of it as an institution both in America and in Africa. He always called Africans "niggers" as a sign of his contempt.

By the end of the last century power politics had spread to Africa. The European powers were not always anxious to take the responsibility for huge new tracts of land in the wilds of Africa, but they were drawn into the scramble by jealousy of one another. At first the spread into the interior was generally left to chartered companies such as the Italian Benadir Company, the British East Africa Company, the German East Africa Company, the Portuguese Companhia de Mocambique and the Belgian Association Internationale du Congo.

The most famous of all these was Cecil Rhodes's South Africa Chartered Company. He had already made a fortune from Kimberley diamonds and the newly discovered gold of the Transvaal; he had also entered politics and become Prime Minister of the Cape Colony. The new Chartered Company was an attempt to combine the two interests of his life by opening up the northern interior to British power and commercial enterprise. The result was the acquisition of what is still Southern Rhodesia and what were once Northern Rhodesia and Nyasaland. Rhodes's cruelty and duplicity in tricking the Matabele and Mashonas into submission were shameful; the present rulers of Southern Rhodesia are faithful imitators of their hero.

At the start of the nineteenth century the white settlers in Africa were confined to the tiny Boer community at the Cape. In 1820 they were joined by about five thousand Englishmen who brought new evangelical ideas on the proper treatment of natives. The Boers, who believed in using the blacks as slaves, decided to break away, and in 1834 they began the famous trek into what are now the Orange Free State, the Transvaal and Natal.

A century later the whites were established all over the great central plateau from South Africa to Kenya. Thanks to the discovery of gold and diamonds, the Transvaal itself became a major industrial civilization. The agreeable climate of Southern Rhodesia had brought thousands of immigrants from South Africa and Britain. Meanwhile rich copper deposits had been found in what was then Northern Rhodesia and in Katanga. Towns like Ndola and Elisabethville had grown into European communities. Even the Portuguese had ventured to settle the interior after four centuries of neglect. They had brought in settlers from the home country to grow coffee or cashew nuts in northern Angola and Mozambique. Above all, the whites trooped into the highlands of Kenya. Throughout the twenties disgruntled ex-soldiers, rebellious second sons, and adventurers of both sexes came to settle the beautiful valleys by the equator. It was not always easy going. Throughout the depression years of the thirties the banks were mean with their credit, and a drop in prices often meant bankruptcy. But the ablest and toughest farmers made a go of it and, after the Second World War, generally found themselves growing rich from increased prices for coffee.

There are less than four million white people in black Africa. More than three million of these are in the Republic of South Africa itself. In this book I have set out to give my impressions of how these white people live, why they want to stay in Africa, how they get on with their black fellow countrymen, and what they hope or fear about the future. During the summer of '64 I visited fourteen countries south of the Sahara in the following order: Kenya, Tanganyika, Southern Rhodesia, Northern Rhodesia (now Zambia), the Congo (former Belgian), Southern Rhodesia (again), South Africa, Mozambique, Angola, the Congo (former French), Chad, Niger, the Ivory Coast, Senegal, and Gambia. Most of the journey was made with the photographer John Bulmer for the *Sunday Times Colour Magazine*, which published an article based on this book in the autumn of '64. Later I visited Ethiopia and Uganda.

Most writers on Africa have to declare a special interest. They are often fanatical pro-whites or pro-blacks. I can claim to have started my first trip to the continent with no particular prejudice either way (indeed this was probably why the *Sunday Times* selected me for the assignment). If anything, my prejudices were rather pro-white, in reaction to the hysterical liberalism of some of my London friends. By the end of the journey my views were slightly pro-black and in favor of Africa for the Africans. This does not mean that I am antiwhite. Politically I disliked the Southern Rhodesians and most South Africans. Fascism in Angola is not better than Fascism in Portugal. On the other hand there is much to admire about the Europeans in most of the independent countries.

I hope I have avoided most of the built-in dangers of writing about Africa. The worst of these lies in trying to be funny about things that are not funny. This is the besetting sin of Evelyn Waugh's books, *Scoop* and *Black Mischief*, which are otherwise very true to modern

Africa. The drunken mercenary, General Connolly, and his wife, "Black Bitch," still haunt the bars of Elisabethville. The United Republic of Tanganyika and Zanzibar has actually thought of calling itself Azania, like the country in Waugh's book. Strangest of all, in Ethiopia recently, two English women propagandists against cruelty to animals were actually fired upon during an insurrection. The white reporters in Africa today are as odd as those in *Scoop*, flying through vulture-infested skies, swimming through shark-infested seas and dodging poisoned arrows to bring you their stories. One *Daily Express* man in the Congo received a cable from London: "ACCORDING TODAYS MAIL MAILMAN YOUNGHUSBAND SHOT AT STOP WHY YOU NOT SHOT AT QUERY." It is easy to laugh at the absurdities of the Congo but one should not laugh at its cruelties. Several journalists recently have been shot at—and hit. Nor is apartheid funny.

Another danger lies in becoming racially conscious. Many people pride thmselves on being "color-blind" and mixing equally well with people of all races. They are seldom as color-blind as they think. In the first place it is much easier to mix socially with people of one's own background, language or culture. An English visitor to East Africa will find much more to talk about with the English there than with the Africans, quite apart from the fact that many Africans there are also reserved and sometimes hostile to whites. I met many white people in Africa who complained that the Africans were stand-offish, and that they behave as the English so often behave to black visitors in their country. The few white people who deliberately mix mostly with Africans frequently develop a kind of racialism turned inwards against themselves. These submerged racial tensions apply much less in West Africa, where people are often genuinely color-blind. But the writer is always tempted either to identify himself too much with the whites or to turn on them too harshly in a frenzied attempt to be fair.

At the end of the book I shall venture a few general ideas on the future of the whites in black Africa. Otherwise this is a piece of reporting, and I have tried to exclude prejudice. Naturally, if certain people and places appear unfavorably, this means that they struck me unfavorably. But these are reactions to circumstance rather than preconceived attitudes.

Kenya

UHURU ("FREEDOM") did not sweep the white men off the streets of Nairobi, as some of the settlers predicted. It has most effectively swept him out of the street directory. The majestic Delamere Avenue, named after the wild white father of Kenya, is now Kenyatta Avenue. The lesser streets, once named after lesser colonial administrators, now celebrate lesser African patriots or Mau Mau brigands. The streets are as clean and neat as ever under the British. The bougainvillaea, golden shower, jacaranda, and scarlet hibiscus remain as proof of one of the finest park departments in the world. I remarked on this to a white Kenyan, not knowing that here, even to praise the look of a city is likely to sound provocative. "Let's hope it stays that way," he said. "If it looks good, that's thanks to the colonialists, the imperialist scum—isn't that what they called us?"

The history of the whites in Kenya has been short, violent and rancorous. The Portuguese had reached the port of Malindi in 1498 and built Fort Jesus at Mombasa by the end of the following century. But the Arabs later regained control over the coast, and few white men had ventured into the interior until the 1890s. On the face of it, this is puzzling. The highlands of Kenya are far more healthy for Europeans than the west coast of Africa; and the land is remarkably fertile. But until the Suez Canal was finished in 1869 this east coast was remote and uninviting. Moreover, the pastoral tribes of Kenya, such as the tall Masai, were a bloodthirsty and brave foe.

The British moved into up-country Kenya from mixed motives of greed and humanitarianism. The Imperial British East Africa Company, formed in 1888, wanted to open up commerce, while the Liberal Government wanted to stamp out the Arab slave trade. Both were also anxious to counteract German influence in nearby Tanganyika. They built a railway line from Mombasa into Uganda—the source of most of the slaves—using Indian coolie labor shipped from Bombay. The town of Nairobi began as a halt on this line at the turn of the century and for many years to come it was little more than a few sheds. Meanwhile some Englishmen, like Lord Delamere, pioneered with farming the beautiful Rift Valley which runs north and south to the west of Nairobi. They became entranced with the idea of making this into a White Highlands, more than 5,000 feet above sea level, on the very edge of the equator.

The British Raj in India had always refused Europeans the right to buy and cultivate land. This rule had been enforced with the idea that the whole subcontinent would one day attain self-government. It was a sound rule and should have been put into force in Kenya. But in the early days of the century, in the Wild West atmosphere of Kenya, there were few people reflective enough to consider the distant future. By the end of the First World War 9,000 whites had settled in Kenya and had taken over most of the best highlands. A Crown Lands Ordinance was passed, allowing the governor of the colony to grant or lease more land as he thought fit. Although, in 1923, the Conservative Government announced the "paramountcy" of African interests, Lord Delamere and the other white leaders had already begun to demand, and achieve, some independence of Whitehall. When London tried to include Arabs and Indians in the legislative council—this was long before anyone considered Africans—the settlers threatened to kidnap the governor.

The first few Africans acquired votes in 1952, which was also the first year of Mau Mau. From then on the colony slithered at breakneck speed towards independence. The whites made a stubborn attempt to keep down the Africans, who outnumbered them more than 100 to 1, and in 1953 they rioted outside Government House in Nairobi. When Sir Michael Blundell returned from a conference at Lancaster House in 1960, having agreed to further advance for the Africans, a white man at the airport presented him with thirty pieces of silver. Even the liberal whites, like Blundell, were pained and bewildered by the velocity of the "wind of change."

Everything in Nairobi was just as I had imagined it from record and legend. I had booked at the Norfolk Hotel, but there was still no room. This had happened to Laurens Van der Post, among other travelers. The cold, self-serve lunch at the New Stanley was just as described in the novels of Robert Ruark. Indeed, this American's two Kenyan sagas, *Something of Value* and *Uhuru*, come up continually in all discussions about the white population. The first novel, set in the time of Mau Mau, tells how a brave, handsome, carefree young Kenyan white has his life shattered by the horrors of the "Emergency." He himself uses black magic and torture to fight the Mau Mau; his health breaks, he takes to drink, and his wife takes off. The second novel, which brings in almost the same characters under different names, continues the psychological torments of the whites into the time of African self-government before independence.

Most Kenyan whites think that Ruark has given a fair and accurate picture of their country. He certainly gives a flattering picture of the whites: the old settlers who defied the tsetse fly and leopard—and bank manager—to bring civilization into the bush; the girl who can tend a sick calf, shoot from the hip, but still give sexual bliss at Mombasa on honeymoon; and the white hunter, symbol of Ruark's hero worship, who can kill with knife, spear or rifle, speak three or four native dialects, read the news of the wild from a bent blade of grass and who, when back in Nairobi, plays sire to the adoring air hostesses.

Although Ruark's books are on sale in Kenya, he himself is banned for having described one of Kenya's present cabinet ministers as a former Mau Mau detainee. The man had never been detained, whatever his sympathies may have been, and he therefore had cause to complain of the book. Even some of the white hunters disliked the books. "*Something of Value* wasn't bad," said Terry Matthews, a thickset, fair-haired young man with a sunburned neck and hoarse voice, "but he described Europeans beating Africans and then made the mistake of trying to justify it. Such things can't be justified. Of course, everyone knows that such things went on during the Emergency. But if anyone senior got to hear of it there was trouble." He himself had done four years in the police during the Emergency and had been a hunter for eight years since.

Like most of the ninety white hunters in Kenya, Mr. Matthews is a specialist. "I stipulate that 50 per cent of my trips should be photographic. You get bored with the shooting—well, no, you get fed up with killing things. Even if you don't shoot them yourself, you feel that if you weren't there the other bloke wouldn't be killing them. Most hunters specialize in areas and in categories of hunting. I specialize in films and elephants. I don't think I'll ever get tired of hunting elephants . . . I've been on thirteen films and I've got the fourteenth coming up. Of course, when they're doing a film, the director and top performers generally do a little hunting on their own as well."

I heard more about the economics of hunting from H. C. F. Wilkes, general manager of Ker, Downey and

Selby Safaris Limited, who have fifteen white hunters under loose contract. Business is good as ever: "Taking our particular sort of safari—we don't take packaged tours—I should say the flow was pretty constant," said Mr. Wilkes. "There was a falling off during the Mau Mau period and briefly during the Congo incident, but people who have traveled a lot don't worry much about it. They realize that there's no more insurance peril than in the Southern states, for instance."

The safari-goers fly to Nairobi, where they generally stay a night before continuing on by small plane to the hunting ground. The actual safaris normally last a month and are booked up a year ahead. "It's sometimes difficult to fix things up, because hunters, being professional people, are temperamental and artistic." A chart on the wall of Mr. Wilkes's office gave the names of his forthcoming customers: the chairman of Chrysler, one of the cornflake Kelloggs, an oriental prince. "Eighty to ninety per cent of our clients are North American; the next, a long way behind, the Italians; then the Danish, Germans, the occasional South American, Indian maharajah, Iranian prince and just sometimes an Englishman. Perhaps the English can't put their safaris on expenses like the others . . . The ordinary American couple can spend more in a month on a safari—without blinking an eyelid—than I've ever earned in a year. The basic cost per person is £1,350, plus license, drinks, ammunition and film. You might even have some extra mileage. And, of course, this doesn't include the air fare. They normally bring their own guns, but gun hire is not a big expense. In the figure we quote, you get very high quality: refrigerator, Dunlopillo mattresses, mosquito-proof tents, laundry and lots of servants."

The white hunters have an association. "We're very proud that in thirty-eight years not one client of our association has ever been touched," said Bill Ryan, a veteran. He himself has a deep scar on the right arm enclosed by a gold arm band. "Somebody shot me when I wasn't looking. We were being charged by a rhino. He lost his head and shot me instead." He has the easy confidence and good humor of Kenyans with long experience in the bush. "I don't like hunting elephants. I don't like shooting elephants. It's either very dangerous, which frightens me, or the poor old thing is simply murdered. But I do like shooting buffalo and cats . . . I first went hunting when I was fourteen. I was paid thirty shillings a day, which had to provide two Africans, a wagon and ten oxen . . . And of course the old-timers were hunting all the time to feed the labor and stop the lions from killing the cattle. Now it's harder to get the practice, and a man who wants to become a hunter has to be vetted before getting a license and then do two years' probation in the association."

There is one Pakistani among the white hunters, a charming, generous, burly man with a sense of humor famous through East Africa, and a fine contempt for "some of the New Stanley Hotel hunters who couldn't hunt a f——ing bottle of beer in the hotel." But there are no black hunters as yet. "The educated African who goes to a university wants a white-collar job," said one white hunter. "He wouldn't want a job like mine, not because it's hard work, which it is, but because it's dirty. And the uneducated African hasn't got the social background. A hunter has got to be responsible for the equipment, the vehicle maintenance, and the medical treatment of the group."

Another white hunter said: "I've got two bearers who are quite capable of taking a client into the bush after buffalo. But they're wild savages from the northeast, and they wouldn't know how to drink with the clients, look after their illnesses, and in general amuse them. The educated African, who could do things like that, has never been in the bush . . . And there's something in their psychology that can't face up to a wounded buffalo. They can't make up their minds that here I am and here I mean to stay. And, of course, since they can run much faster than the client, there'd be hell to pay . . . There are a few exceptions, like game rangers, who have all the qualities . . . I've made a point of asking every client for the last few years what his reaction would be to an African hunter, and they all said, 'I wouldn't come.' " However, he thinks that the Kenya Government appreciates the role of the white hunter and his usefulness to the tourist trade, so he sees no danger of being "Africanized."

One danger that has to be faced by the white hunter is the demand for ever greater expertise. The Duke of Edinburgh, for instance, is blamed for the bird-watching fad. A hunter, quoted in *Africana Magazine*, complains: "When I first started this business, all I had to know was how to tell a spoor, how to tell a good head from a bad, a male from a female, and a kitehawk from a Little Brown Bird. Now if I can't tell the difference between a Kklaas Cuckoo and a White-browed Coucal and point out a Golden-rumped Tinker-bird and a Black-headed Gonolek when I see one, I'm likely to lose a client."

Some hunters have acquired a considerable knowledge of cinema and TV from constantly escorting such gentry into the bush. In the novels of Ernest Hemingway—whose son, incidentally, works as a white hunter in Kenya—the client's wife generally slides under the hunter's mosquito net. In the fantasies of the hunters themselves, it is the film actresses.

The romantic white hunters are only a fraction of Kenya's white population, although they probably symbolize the fantasies of the rest. Before *uhuru*, there were 65,000 white settlers. Today there are still nearly 45,000 British in Kenya. The High Commissioner's Office in Nairobi is the largest in the world, after the one in New Delhi. Of these whites, probably more than half still are settlers, earning a living from their own land, and regarding Kenya as their true home. "This is probably the only foreign country," said Sir Geoffrey de Freitas, just before he resigned as High Commissioner, "where the British businessmen—bank managers and merchants—are not the leaders of the British colony. One of the things I've tried to do here is to give greater prestige and support to the business community. This has been made easier by the decline in the political power of the settlers."

Sir Geoffrey had come to Kenya from Ghana, and he

was quite clear which country he preferred. "In Ghana there were fewer whites, no racial prejudice. The Africans were more advanced and therefore more confident. Here in Kenya they tend to be prickly." Even his dog was Ghanaian. It was plain that Sir Geoffrey had had a rough time with some of the more intransigent settlers who would not have been well disposed to a former Labor M.P. "There are still some left. We've still got some crosses to bear. But the worst have gone and good riddance to them . . . The Kenya settlers have always been hostile to the British Government. I've tried to be their ally and friend, but it doesn't come naturally to them."

I told a Nairobi journalist I was doing a story about the white man in Africa. "You've come just in time," he said. It was more than six months since *uhuru*, and although the worst fears of the settlers had not yet been realized, there were rumors of more expulsions. These were to follow soon afterwards. Those who have been here longest seem most determined to stay. "I love this country," said a journalist, "and if they want to get me out they'll have to winkle me out with a bayonet." Characteristically the present Lord Delamere has been co-operating in the settlement of African farmers. Those who have left in a huff were most often the latest arrivals, also the most right-wing and the most vociferous for their "stake in the country."

Before leaving Nairobi for the country, I went to see how integration was getting along in Delamere Girls' High School (motto *Sapere Aude*), whose pupils affect a fetching boater. It is a former hospital laid out in single-story buildings round a courtyard bright with jacarandas and moonflowers. It is a grammar school, not quite so posh as Kenya High, and theoretically integrated. But there are only a handful of African girls. This is a cause of great regret to Miss J. R. Hills, the headmistress, who came out to teach here from London. "There's no public transport. They can't get here, the poor little things. They have to take a bus and then go on foot. The trouble is that the African hasn't got the home background for a grammar-school education. They're so crowded together and haven't got room to do their homework." The expense is another problem. "Fees are only two hundred and ninety shillings a term, but they have a uniform to pay for, which is another stumbling block. Yet I'd be loath to give up the uniform. It's a leveling influence."

She says the African girls have tremendous potential for learning and are some of the best students in the school. One of them is Tom Mboya's cousin and proved a natural leader and "terrifically good at all sports." At assembly that morning Miss Hills announced: "At the netball match yesterday against the Aga Khan's School, your team won 11-9." The applause sounded disproportionate to the size of the victory, and I asked why. Apparently Delamere High seldom wins a match. The children have to play sports during school hours because just as soon as school is ended the parents come in the car to take them away.

"They're very uninhibited, the children here," Miss

Hills remarked. "It's partly because of all the social life. People are able to entertain much more, and the children get used to society. And since children are never left alone in the house—it goes back to the Mau Mau, and there's been a lot of housebreaking recently—the parents take them with them on visits. Sometimes they take the small ones along and leave them in the back of the car while they go to a drink party . . . The girls here are very graceful, especially compared to London. But they get upset very easily. They weep a lot, although I'm not a very fierce person . . . Perhaps it's the altitude . . . A lot of girls now come for two or three years only while their fathers are working over here on contract. It will be a very bad thing for the school when a majority of the girls look on Kenya just as a place where father's working."

Nairobi remains very English—"Would you like your beer cold or warm?" the waiter asked—but the Americans who come to hunt often stay to work or settle. This is typified by the Mount Kenya Safari Club in the foothills of that mountain to the north. The main building and chalets offer accommodation for a hundred of its eight hundred members. Its trimmed lawns, flower beds, swimming pool, miniature golf course and hi-fi piped music can be enjoyed within yards of the equator. There are flocks of ornamental birds—one of which attacked John Bulmer—television and a copy of *Time* in every bedroom. There are pictures by Trebitschev on the walls, and native drums sound at cocktail time from the club's private native village.

The club was founded by William Holden, the film actor, who had made several pictures in Kenya, and by Ray Ryan, an American oil and property millionaire. "There are so many people pulling their money out of Kenya," said the press officer of the club, "and yet there's Ray Ryan pouring God knows how much money into this place." And there, as he spoke, was Ray Ryan in person, wearing a wide cowboy hat and riding clothes, Mexican long boots and a trickle of blood down the left side of the shirt. "It's nothing, just a scratch," he said. Just a wound, he might have said and remained in character.

Some of the locals call the club "the millionaires' drinkery," yet it is not really dear for the standard of comfort. And Mr. Ryan made it clear that "this is not a profit-making club. The principles of the club are the preservation of game and helping children through school." The hundred and fifty Africans on the payroll have a hundred and thirty-five school children. "We clothe them, buy uniforms, feed them and, if they show any promise, help them through higher education."

He and Holden both spend six months of the year at the club. They are confident of the future. "Independence has increased the amount of tourism. The Minister of Tourism, Mr. Uneki, is doing a wonderful job. The stability and forcefulness of Mr. Kenyatta is a stablilizing force." Indeed, Mr. Kenyatta and Mr. Tom Mboya were guests of the club last year and were said to have spent a jovial evening. The trouble, as Mr. Ryan sees it, is that American tourists tend to get worried by trouble anywhere in Africa. "The continent of Africa being as large as it is, people don't realize the distance that exists between Kenya and the Congo, or Kenya and South Africa. East Africa as a whole is among the most stable parts of the continent . . . The Kenya Government rightly welcomes visitors from the English isle and has always been friendly to the Americans."

Nature itself presents problems to the Mount Kenya Safari Club. "We've lost a lot of our birds to leopards—secretary birds, yellow necks, darters. What we're endeavoring to do is to make this an outstanding bird sanctuary . . . We built the bridle paths so that people can go out fishing, and we built barbecue pits so they can eat the fish they caught for lunch. Then there'll be a series of dams which we'll use as hazards for the golf course. We'll have four lakes we'll be shooting over, and we hope to have some pretty good golfers coming here. Arnold Palmer's a member and Sam Snead's a member. Crosby and Hope are also members when you're talking about golf. Of course, our most famous member was Winston Churchill." Other members and guests include several Habsburgs, some Italian nobility, many Americans, several Japanese. Even the most fastidious guests would be satisfied with Mr. Ryan's rules for the kitchen staff. "In the kitchen there's a big disinfectant bowl and a big brush. Everyone that comes into that kitchen has got to scrub his hands each time. And all of them have to have a shower bath each day."

Several days passed in Kenya before I first heard white people using one of the old derogatory words for the blacks. It was beside the pool of the Mount Safari Club, and those concerned were not members but British officers and their wives from the nearby Army camp. "The way some of the coons drive, it's no fun driving any more," said a frowning young wife of an officer. "I nearly ran into the back of some of them the other night on the road to Nairobi. There were three of the silly coons in an Anglia without a single light." The man in a bush hat beside her drawled, "Bloody wogs." The frowning woman relapsed into a study of the newspaper. Evidently her mind was still in the same groove. "Zambia!" she exclaimed, seeing a reference to the future of Northern Rhodesia. "Zambia! Isn't it bloody marvelous?" The man in the bush hat said "Bloody wogs" in the same tone of colossal boredom. There are no people more boring or bored than those obsessed with racial hatred.

Such fragments of rubbish overheard in England would scarcely arouse surprise or concern. They rang strangely in Kenya, where the white people are cautious about their language. In the old colonial days, so it is said, it was normal to talk of niggers, coons or wogs, even in front of Africans. Nowadays the use of such a word would carry the risk of expulsion. When you call the waiter in Kenya it is no longer correct to shout "boy" even though servants will often apply for jobs as "boy." The right word now is "steward." Some Kenyans joke, and the joke is not without seriousness, that one can give offense by asking for coffee black or white. It is better to say with or without. The Army officers and their wives would ignore such conventions when out of black earshot and with only a few months left in the country. The settlers would avoid giving offense, not just out of self-protection but because a large proportion of them have a strict code of manners. The kind of Englishman in Kenya who called the Africans "niggers" is just the kind to have left at the time of *uhuru*.

The club and the Army camp lie on the outskirts of Nanyuki. More than half the Europeans have left this district since independence. Apparently they tend to desert the ranching areas more than the crop farms. Also Nanyuki is temptingly near a big Kikuyu reservation. The farmers can feel these African eyes looking enviously at the land. A young Kenya Scot, whose wife's family owns a local hotel, was of two minds. "Sometimes I feel like staying on. Sometimes I feel like selling the farm and and the hotel and going to Australia. Then, of course, I might sell the farm but stay on here in Kenya. It's the land of the living here. The land of the living."

He found Nanyuki itself very depressing, now that so many Europeans had gone. "There are about a hundred and fifty left, and when they had a play the other night about a hundred and twenty of them turned out. But you never see them the rest of the year." One elderly woman was pleased enough. She had been pensioned off by the British Government on compassionate grounds. She had proved to them that independence made it no longer possible to run her little business or find another. But those without clear reason to leave must find someone to buy their farm. And here there are no buyers.

The Nanyuki Hunt, founded in 1942, was holding its

last meet. The Army, which had created it and cared for the pack of hounds, was due to leave in the autumn. "We normally meet once a week," said Major Sir Torquhil Matheson, an immense mustachioed man in Master's pink, "but we've been rather having a go of it recently because this is the last month." There used to be five hunts in Kenya. When the Nanyuki stopped, there would be only two. There were twenty-five horses this morning and hounds led by an African whip, also in uniform, "who could lead the hunt himself." They hunt here in the rainy season for reed buck, jackals and sometimes bush buck, but these are rather difficult, as they disappear into the undergrowth. The meet was outside the schoolhouse. There was coffee or Bols as a stirrup cup and much hearty talk about the parties the previous night, for in Kenya they hunt on a Sunday.

The horn toots. The pink-coated, red-faced master of hounds digs in his spurs. The pink-coated, black-faced whip cracks the thong over the hounds. The ladies in jodhpurs shout back the last Swahili instructions to the servants guarding the children. The horses neigh their challenge over the bush. The cloud lifts off Mount Kenya and, apparently, two hundred yards away, a bush buck has bolted from hiding. It is ridiculous, I suppose, and an anachronism, but rather magnificent all the same.

The same young Scot who disliked Nanyuki spoke enviously of the Europeans in the Subukia Valley, to the west: "They're a very happy crowd. They don't moan and groan about the Government. In the Subukia Club if you talk politics you're asked to leave. Very few people have gone from the Subukia Valley." It was difficult to find estimates of how many had actually gone. By the middle of 1964 it was still as few as three families out of a hundred. "Three years ago," said one Subukia resident, "some friends of ours had a fancy dress ball and they were saying, "Oh, we'll never have one of these again." They came to stay last weekend, and we went over the invitation list of three years back. Only two families were not still around. One weren't really farmers anyway. The others were dead."

There was no shortage of guests at the wedding held in the church at Subukia during my stay. The bridegroom came from Nanyuki, and most of his guests had broken the drive at Thompson's Falls to change in the hotel. They went upstairs wearing the typical Kenyan bush jackets and came down in their wedding best. The young women looked prettier in their bush clothes than in the unaccustomed, unfashionable dresses and hats. The men kept fingering their ties (often Old Wellingtonian or Guards) with the air of people not used to wearing them. Nor had there been time for a proper bath or wash after the long drive over dusty, red murram roads—so that most of the guests had an earthy look.

The wedding itself, according to the guests, was "just like old times." The tiny stone church had room for only a few of the guests. The rest stood chatting outside beside the cars. People from distant farms greeted old friends they had not seen for months; "How's settlement going down your way?" meaning settlement of the

Africans on to their own farms. "Pathetic. Labor I thought was loyal has gone absolutely to pot."

On the hill above the road a small group of Africans stood watching the scene in silence. "They've come to take a good look at us before they take our farms," said one of the guests. It was one of those jokes that do not have a funny ring.

"The bride and bridegroom are very horsy," one of the guests explained, and sure enough they left the church under an arch of crossed polo sticks held by two plump girls on horseback. The confetti must have startled the animals, for they shied, breaking the arch, just as the young couple appeared. "Daniel, be decent!" the bridegroom said to one of the horses, and "Get your heels in!" he said to the girls. The couple went away in a horse and cart whose coachman wore top hat, redingote and all. The whole thing earned the approval of one rather tough-looking lady guest. "I'm a policewoman in Northern Rhodesia," she said, " . . . a marvelous country. Polo and parties and hunting. I'll stay there until they throw us out."

Afterwards came the reception with champagne under a hot sun, followed by smaller parties in many a farm along the valley. "You're going to say what an idle lot we white settlers are," said one of the friends of the bride; "you'll think we spend all our time drinking. It's like that time there were about ten of us sitting around on the floor, rather drunk, listening to the record player, when somebody brought in this Clerk to the Council of Norfolk or Suffolk or somewhere. This man says that it's always fun to come in at the end of a party, which was rather an unfortunate remark really, because the party was only just beginning." A swaying man said over and over again, "Do you know who I am? I'm the black sheep of the family." "When my daughter got married," another guest said, "we had some Africans in for a glass of champagne, and they thought it was marvelous. I notice there aren't any Africans here today, but it's got to come. We've got to mix." The Scotsman from Nanyuki was most impressed by it all. "In Subukia everyone drinks and is jolly. They go on drinking till morning and then stagger out to play tennis! This is really the land of the living . . ."

Like the Highlanders of Scotland, the White Highlanders of Kenya have adopted separate clan identities from the valleys in which they live. The most famous clan of all before the war were the people who lived in what was called Happy Valley to the southeast of the Subukia. They earned this nickname from their lighthearted indulgence in adultery. Other valleys had a reputation for hot blood and violent politics. Most of these clans, including the people of Happy Valley, had been dispersed by African settlement. The Subukia, richest and loveliest of them all, has not yet been touched by the Kenya Government. This may be because it produces very good cash crops: coffee, tea, pyrethrum (the basis of insecticide), besides excellent beef and dairy herds. If divided up into small holdings, the land would certainly lose its value in exports and therefore in profit to the Kenyan Exchequer. Some old hands scent an even more subtle reason for their continued presence here. The Subukia Valley lies along the border between the Kikuyu and the Kalenjin tribes, old enemies from before the days of the British and now divided by politics. It may be that Jomo Kenyatta sees the British as a convenient cushion between his own Kikuyu and KANU Party, and the hostile Kalenjin and KADU. The British mostly support KADU as well, but they are hardly likely to start up tribal war.

Sir Michael Blundell, the long-time settlers' leader who at last persuaded the angry whites to accept the inevitability of black rule, still lives in his retirement in the Subukia Valley. I asked him why the valley had thus far enjoyed such an amicable relationship with the independent Kenyan Government. "The people here have always been more liberal than the rest of the settlers. At least 90 per cent of them used to vote for me until Lancaster House [where Sir Michael in 1960 virtually agreed to the end of settler rule]; and even after Lancaster House about 60 per cent voted for me. Most of them are older-generation settlers and get on well with Africans. The new people who came out after the war were the kind that couldn't adapt to a Labor Government. And if they couldn't adapt to a Labor Government, how the hell could they hope to adapt to Africa?"

After a tough life in farming and politics, Sir Michael has now retired, whether willingly or not, to "cultivate his garden." And this is quite literally how he passes the time. The box hedges, the ornamental pool and the serried beds of flowers make this a tidy patch of Hampshire in Africa. Like so many Kenyans, Sir Michael is full of apparent contradictions. With his plump, burly frame and broad, red face, let alone the name Blundell, he seems a caricature of a right-wing, roast-beef Briton abroad. Yet, in his late twenties, Sir Michael studied in Germany to be a professional *lieder* singer. A farmer and soldier with exactly the same background as the most of his fellow settlers, he had the guts to take an unpopular liberal line in the dark days before independence. He was a KADU supporter and hostile to Jomo Kenyatta in politics; but he is one of the very few Europeans claiming—and I believe him—that he actually likes the Kikuyu. His farm and garden are among the finest in Africa, yet he advanced the idea, with philosophical resignation, that the British had introduced too advanced a level of scientific agriculture to be compatible with the life of Africa. He seemed to suggest that the settlers would have to go and the land regress to primitive agriculture before it could start to progress again at an African pace. For a man like Blundell and many fellow white Kenyans who have worked and love the land, this is a sad prospect. But they face it with calm.

In Kenya any eccentricity gets blamed on the altitude. In his recent autobiography, Sir Michael suggested the theory that settler tempers were more inflamed at 8,000 than at 6,000 feet. His own farm is at 7,500, which may explain Sir Michael's vivacity. No sooner had I arrived than I was driven off to see his pyrethrum plantation and then taken for a plunge into the forest to look at Kolobus monkeys. He could pick out these animals among the foliage from an extraordinary distance. Talking politics in the dining room with after-lunch coffee, he suddenly remembered the Test match and insisted on bringing in a transistor radio to hear the play. When the drawl of the commentator's voice began to grate, even on Sir Michael's nerves, he dispatched Lady Blundell with the radio into the drawing room with instructions to poke her head round the door if any wickets fell.

One expects to hear liberal sentiments from Sir Michael Blundell. But like most English visitors to Kenya, I was astonished by the quite widespread feeling of goodwill toward independent Kenya among ordinary European farmers. "Where are are the reactionaries?" I found myself asking once. "You mean the 'red eyes'? That's what we call them. There weren't very many of them anyway, and now they've mostly gone. Good riddance to them." I quote below some observations on politics taken almost at random from farmers in the Subukia Valley, all of whom would probably vote Conservative back in Britain.

An elderly man with a north-country grammar-school background: "I think the Africans are going to get their land in the end. It's inevitable. But they've got to farm it in larger areas. And I think the top people realize that. As long as Jomo's there, it will be all right. Jomo's really wonderful . . . A friend of mine works in a bank giving loans to African farmers, and it's his job to go down and see who's capable of using the money properly. He says a lot of the Africans are very good. Of course, they'll make mistakes. After all, they've got to make mistakes before they learn. And then a lot of European farmers weren't very good either . . . A lot of people blame the British Government, but I don't agree with them as long as the British help us out if things go wrong here."

A former Special Branch officer in the Emergency, and a supporter of Blundell: "The official line about Mau Mau is to let bygones be bygones. I got a lot of threatening letters immediately before independence, and verbal threats in the towns. I thought I'd get the chop in retribution, but I've heard nothing since . . . After Lancaster House, when I was helping Michael Blundell and giving speeches to Africans in Kiswahili, I was beaten up one night in the Rift Club, kicked downstairs by people who said I was an African lover. And I do like Africans. You can do anything with an African as long as you're fair and you treat him as a human being" . . . Some people had been annoyed when Kenyatta said that whites should learn to call Africans "Bwana." "The word 'bwana' just means mister. In some tribes they all call each other Bwana. Lots of Europeans say, 'I'll be damned if I'll call an African Bwana.' But I say it's simply politeness, and the African is very polite . . . It's all right here while Kenyatta and the other responsible people are in power —people who are trying to do something for Kenya. But if they go, the ignorant and irresponsible people will take over, and you've no idea how bloody irresponsible and bloody ignorant most of them are . . . People in England say we slave-drive the Africans, but, my God, it's the other way round. You come back dog-tired in the evening, and they start coming up to you: somebody's stolen my wife, somebody's raped my daughter, my eyes hurt, I want a new pair of trousers . . . Unlike England, where everything you see has been built by your great-grandfather, everything you see here has been built by yourself. I'll tell you one thing this does: it makes you bloody loath to leave."

A former naval officer: "I'm an official of KADU, and lots of people round here used to think me beyond the pale. Look at old X over there. Two years ago he wouldn't even speak to me. He thought I was the scum of the earth. Now he wants to stay in Kenya—and we get on all right together . . . If all the Europeans pulled out overnight there'd be chaos, because the Africans would rush into grab the land they thought was theirs . . . But if the Europeans think that by holding the country up to ransom in that way they're going to get anywhere, they're wrong . . . Besides, most of the Europeans, even if they haven't got wealthy, have had a very nice time. And if you have that you owe something to the country."

A farmer's wife: "We've been here thirty-eight years and we couldn't adapt to any other environment. All our friends are here, and I'd rather have my throat cut here than retire in England . . . We've all got used to Africans in the clubs and the restaurants. Those who couldn't get used to it have gone back and good riddance to them . . . Everyone who has met Jomo speaks tremendously highly of him. He's courteous, punctual, considerate, and by far the best Minister to deal with. I don't know where we'd be without him. And to think that only eighteen months ago we were thinking how we could manage to shoot the bastard. I think the English must have got at him in prison and brainwashed him. You know, at first they gave him cases of brandy and tried to get him to drink himself to death. But he resisted, which speaks well for his strength of character."

The volatile, white Kenyans came round within a year from regarding Jomo Kenyatta as the devil incarnate to making him a father-figure. They talk about him, unblushingly, in the kind of fulsome language that Soviet writers once used of Stalin. "Jomo has exceeded our wildest dreams," said one man. "That's why Jomo's so marvelous. He does what he says he would," came another tribute. "Wasn't it wonderful the way Jomo rewrote the national anthem!" a lady gushed. And this is how a former militant right-winger described his first encounter with Mr. Kenyatta: "He was extremely courteous. In fact, he was waiting outside his house. I'd heard all the stories about his physical appearance—the blubbery lips and cruel eyes and so on—so I made a special point of looking into his eyes. I thought this is an old man but a kind man. I said so afterwards, and everyone said, 'My God, you haven't let yourself be fooled by that old devil, have you?' So I said, 'All right. I've been fooled by Baring [a former Governor] and I've been fooled by Blundell. Now I've been fooled by Kenyatta.' "

Most of the European farmers were born in Kenya or have lived there most of their lives. "Where else can I go? This is my home," is the stock remark about the future. One young couple had made all their plans for moving to South Africa, but thought there was little more safety there. "If I'm going to be nyonga'd over the head," the woman said, "I'd rather be nyonga'd in the place I've lived in all my life than in one I don't know." If they talk of leaving Kenya, it is seldom Britain they think of going to. One or two mentioned Australia or Ethiopia, but more often South Africa. Generally there was little political significance in this. Several people said they disliked the way the South Africans treated the natives, or they disliked the Afrikaners or they disliked the English South Africans. One man came up with the totally untrue story that in South Africa, when a sexy film is released, it is shown at separate cinemas for men and women. These Kenyans think of going to South Africa not because it is racialistic but because it is one part of Africa where they could live out their days. Most of all they would like to continue living in Kenya.

Again and again the farmers hark back to the fact that they have created the farms with their own toil. "On the place where you're standing, sixteen years ago there was absolutely nothing. It was just thorn and bush. There were elephants and a few lions and any amount of leopards. Now there are four thousand acres under cultivation, and either I'm a good farmer or I'm a complete fool, because I've put every bean I've got into this farm. To give you some idea, I put in £25,000 in one year during the Emergency. And the place still hasn't paid off." The old-timers who lived here during the Mau

Mau terror feel particularly unwilling to go now. "I spent years with a revolver in my hand, quite literally in my hand, because it was unsafe to leave it anywhere," said one mild, middle-aged man. Once only I left it in the other room by mistake, and the butler brought it in on a silver tray with a solemn look on his face." Oddly enough the Europeans are far from eager to talk about Mau Mau days, although the experience offered everyone the material to bore friends and acquaintances for life. This may be partly owing to a reluctance to boast of their bravery in the past. It may be that they share with the Kikuyu a wish to forget the dreadful episode. Some of the whites retaliated against the Mau Mau with shameful brutality. For the more sensitive it is a time of unpleasant memories.

Anyone who has traveled widely in Africa by car or on foot must have remarked on the general friendliness of the blacks. They will usually smile, wave, or shout a greeting. In the White Highlands of Kenya this is not the case. The Africans quite often throw stones at the cars. A white driver involved in a road accident is likely to get beaten or worse. The faces along the roadside stare and scowl in a way that makes long drives rather depressing. The white Kenyans acknowledge that they do not get on well with the Kikuyu. Nor, when it comes to that, do most of the other African tribes. The Kikuyu believe, rightly or wrongly, that the whites have taken their land; the whites in turn depended on the Kikuyu as the Africans most suited to agricultural work.

Here are some of the commonest attitudes of the

whites toward their fellow Kenyans. They tend to think the Kikuyu humorless, untrustworthy, avaricious, cruel, and devoted to sorcery. Of course, every single settler who makes these generalizations will immediately come up with a long list of exceptions, often beginning with his personal cook or houseboy, "who was completely loyal throughout the Emergency." This hostility to the Kikuyus—which was, of course, greatly increased by the Emergency—is matched by different degrees of affection for all the other tribes. The Kalenjin tribes, such as the Kipsigis, are popular, although they are not usually such able workers as the Kikuyu. And all whites adore the Masai, the gigantic nomadic warriors who live off blood drained from living cattle. One soon gets bored with stories (see the novels of Robert Ruark) of valiant Masais scattering treacherous, cowardly Kikuyu. "They're marvelous people. People who live here get completely Masai-ized," said one man who was himself Masaiized.

It is easy to explain this affection as hypocritical preference for the tribe that does not stand up for its own rights or independence. Certainly many white Kenyans "like the savages well enough as long as they stay savage." There is a streak of paternalism mixed with the kind of patronizing goodwill that English aristocrats show towards working-class people who "know their place." Indeed, one Subukia aristocrat said, "The real nigger hater has gone out with the ark. The educated African is anathema to me, but I like the sort who is a houseboy or a poacher." A very few of the settlers get on really well with the Kikuyu, know their ways and are, in turn, trusted. Even those who dislike them most have a grudging respect for their intelligence. One phrase I heard several times from the Europeans, and it was said with admiration, was, "You've got to admit the Kukes were one jump ahead of us all the time."

There is a violence and exuberance about the white Kenyans which recalls the age of Tom Jones. One of the most pro-African of the whites I met admitted that he quite frequently beat his servants. When one of his several dogs howled too loudly he cheerfully kicked its head in a way that would horrify kindly people in England. Yet he is not a cruel man. He and his wife are extremely friendly with Africans—"I felt at home immediately I came out here. The Africans are so like the Irish"—and indeed he himself is rather African in his outlook. A neighbor recalled, "We had a cockfight in the drawing room one night. When my wife got back there were blood and feathers all over the place. She was furious." No wonder.

The Kenyan whites are notorious for their sexuality. All the world knows the joke question, "Are you married or do you live in Nairobi?" Whether the town and the country still live up to their reputation it would take a Kinsey report to decide. Certainly the divorce rate is quite high. Certainly conversation is quite uninhibited about sex. Certainly many Kenyan women, right into late middle age, have a look in the eye which registers to the male that they have not lost interest. And certainly, almost needless to say, all adultery is blamed on the altitude.

This does not mean that the white Kenyans are boorish. Continually one is astonished by their sprightly interest in their world and the world outside, by their willingness to adapt to new ideas and conditions. Many of them probably came to Kenya as rebels or misfits or discontented second sons or simply from love of adventure. This attitude of mind, at its best, is well suited to meeting difficulties. "It's a pity it may have to end," they often say, "but we had a good time while it lasted." There is something admirable about people who can so cheerfully pack their bags just at the time of life when others expect to retire and enjoy the fruits of work.

Patriotic Africans in Kenya often wear ties commemorating *uhuru*. Some of the whites have bought them, too, with quite unpolitical motives. "Honestly, I'm going to get myself a *uhuru* tie. With one of those round your neck you can sail through the customs," one of them joked. A few whites in Kenya, including Lord Delamere, have taken the more serious step of acquiring Kenyan citizenship. One of them told me, "There was a lot of jingoistic talk about not giving up one's British passport. Well I've done so, and it's a pretty painless process. All I did was to swear an oath of allegiance to Her Majesty Queen Elizabeth II . . . so help me God. And if I want my British passport back I can get it pretty easily." A more cautious and conservative Englishman said he was thinking of doing the same, but "at the moment it would look like a loss of face and wouldn't really impress the African. After all, he knows perfectly well that we're not one of them." And a young third-generation white Kenyan said, "If I became a Kenyan citizen I might be liable for service in the Kenyan Army and made to fight the South Africans. And I don't want to fight the South Africans. Whatever you may think of the South Africans, they're doing more for the Africans than anybody else. And yet I think there's a great future for the white man in this country, as long as they don't bugger us about."

That is the question. Most of the white farmers think that some of their number will have to go. Some fear that all will go. "The fewer of us there are, the better things will be," said one of the most canny farmers in the Subukia Valley. The pessimists argue that Kenya's future lies in the tourist industry, that a healthy tourist industry needs a stable political situation and that a stable political situation can come only when the Africans have satisfied their land hunger. Everyone seems to fear the ex-Mau Mau extremists waiting to seize power. "I mean, at the moment you've got Jomo," said a charming Kenyan lady, "but what would happen if the poor old dear conked out? In Africa you never have a clue about the future."

Tanganyika and Uganda

THE WHITE MAN in Africa tends to extremes of optimism or pessimism about his future, and to extreme credulity about what is happening to his fellows in neighboring countries. In East Africa two years ago the white Kenyans feared they were going to be thrown out of their farms, or worse, as soon as the gong went for *uhuru*. When everything turned out better than they had expected there was an immediate 180-degree swing to excessive faith in the Government of Mr. Kenyatta. There was a corresponding swing in attitude towards Tanganyika. This country, which the British took from the Germans as a protectorate after the First World War, had never been settled much by the whites, and there was consequently no jealousy about land—and, therefore, no Mau Mau. Much as the whites feared Jomo Kenyatta, they considered their future was safe under the wise, kindly Julius Nyerere. Even Robert Ruark, speaking through one of his characters, throws out a word of praise for the future rulers of Tanganyika. This mood lasted until January, 1964, when the Tanganyikan

Army rose against its officers, and Zanzibar had its cruel revolution. The Kenya of Jomo Kenyatta now seemed the more stable country for white people. It was Julius Nyerere and his colleague Oscar Kambona who took over the mantle of odium from the suddenly blessed Kenyatta.

Many white Kenyans warned us against Tanganyika. "That's the country I wouldn't care to be in just now," was one typical comment. "There are so many Cubans there they've had to build three more blocks of flats for them on the sea front. And they do the goose step everywhere. Even the man who comes onto the plane at the airport to spray the Flit does the goose step. Even the children do the goose step." I noted down these other warnings with the comment, "I'll believe that when I see it." And, of course, the rumors were quite false. There are at the most three Cubans in Tanganyika, whatever their influence on Zanzibar. Any new blocks of flats on the waterfront could be hastily snapped up by the richer Western embassies or by the Tanganyikan Government. Nobody came on to spray the plane at a Tanganyika airport, nor did I see any sign of a goose step from anyone, whether official, soldier, adult or child. The Tanganyikan Army was still in disgrace after the mutiny, and the only troops in evidence were the smart and well-disciplined Nigerians who had been brought in to keep order. They retain the easy British step in the march.

The heat and damp give Dar es Salaam an air of sweet decay which strikes African after the brisk highlands of Kenya. The plaster rots, the tin rusts, and damp spreads like a stain over the side of the new flats. A cooking fire blazes in the third-story tenement opposite. The mood is of working-class Athens or middle-class Bombay. It is far less British than Kenya. In Margot's excellent restaurant the dandified French-trained African headwaiter suggests, "Why don't you try our Tournedos Stroganov. It's Madame's creation, and I think I can guarantee that you'll go away rejuvenated." The multiracial jukebox bars are a far cry from the solemn strip club of Nairobi. Two Liberians, two Germans and their girls chat in English. Then the girls break into a fight. The argument is yelled in Swahili, but the final insults are yelled in English. "You fuckee bush girl!" It is a very agreeable city.

Racial relations are not good, as I saw from one trivial incident on the first day in Dar es Salaam. A group of seven French sailors on their way to have a drink at the New Africa Hotel were stopped by a beggar woman with a baby. One of the sailors took her photograph, but apparently they rather meanly refused her a handout. The woman got angry and followed the sailors into the lounge of the New Africa, which opens onto the street. She continued to ask for money, and the sailors continued to shrug her off with embarrassed grins. The beggar woman called a policeman and a policewoman, who in turn began to remonstrate with the sailors. It was no longer a question of money but of having taken the woman's photograph without her permission. The foolish sailors, who did not want to appear soft in front of each other, maintained a stubborn indifference. A crowd began to collect on the veranda outside, and there was angry shouting. Finally the policeman ordered the sailors to go to the station. Alarmed at last, they insisted on seeing the French Consul in an office block across the street. A crowd jostled them as they went up and again as they came out. For nearly two hours the argument continued at the consulate, in the street, and back in the hotel. At last the sailors went along to the police station for a reprimand. The watching crowd was extremely hostile to the sailors, and I feared at one time that there might be violence. "Foreigners must learn how to behave in Tanganyika," said a rather pompous, nattily dressed man wearing the characteristic, saucer-sized dark glasses of Africa.

There have been many similar incidents. Some English guests at a Dar es Salaam hotel were ignominiously expelled because they had failed to stand up when the visiting President of Guinea passed through the lounge. Their no doubt quite justified protest that they had not recognized him was brushed aside with irritation. There were two state visits during our stay which demanded the utmost respect from blacks and whites alike. Our car was kept waiting for twenty minutes at the side of the road out of deference to the President of the Republic, who was expected in a motorcade from the other direction. Some Europeans deliberately court trouble by calculated insult to the susceptibilities of the régime. One can sympathize with the Ghanaian authorities for having expelled the British journalist who did not stand up at the national anthem.

Racial tension is worse for the Arabs and Asiatics. The former found several dead during the riots that followed the mutiny. The latter, caught as ever between the whites and the blacks, have quickly learned to recognize who is the new master. There was a good example of this in the small Indian-managed hotel where John Bulmer and I had taken rooms. One night at about three A.M., Bulmer woke to find that two very drunk and bemused Africans had blundered into his room. He shooed them out, locked the door and went back to sleep. About half an hour later he was woken up again by the smell of burning and found that billows of smoke were coming in from the corridor and ultimately from the room next door, which was locked. With the help of a porter, Bulmer broke down the door and found that the two drunks had dozed off to sleep leaving a bed on fire. They extinguished it. But the spree was not over. Half an hour later Bulmer was woken a third time by screams and banging. The irrepressible revelers had recovered enough to invite a girl to their room and then apparently had pitched her into the corridor practically naked. The next morning we spoke to the Indian manager about the events of the night. We said, rather primly, that we sincerely hoped the troublesome neighbors had left the hotel. The manager, poor fellow, looked embarrassed. No, they had not gone yet. But was he not going to evict them? No, said the manager, they would not go "until the conference is over." And so the truth came out. The merrymakers were delegates of the TANU ruling political party, and it was therefore more than the manager's job was worth to complain. The moral of this story is amusing. Before independence any complaint by Englishmen would probably have had the guests removed very promptly. Now it was the Africans who can "throw their race about," so to speak. As always, it is the Indians who suffer.

The British are by far the largest element in the European community and by far the most distinctive. Most of the men in banks, business or technical assistance wear the old colonial rig of white shirt, white shorts and white stockings. They frequently stick the stem of their pipe down the side of the stocking with just the bowl peeping over the edge. I have noticed as many as three pipes in one stocking. Most of the British are cool or even hostile towards the new Tanganyika Government. "The Government doesn't mind young Europeans coming here, but they want to get rid of us old-timers," said a former colonial servant. "We know too much about them. I know, for example, that four of the Government have been in prison for theft, including one for armed robbery." A woman followed up the same theme: "Of course, I first knew [Minister X] when I had an office above the law court and he was brought in for libel, although I think they called it sedition." Then again, "Nyerere lives in State House, what used to be the Governor's Palace. But, of course, when the Governor lived there the doors were always open. Now there are iron gates and barbed wire outside." Many British people in Dar es Salaam claim to know all kinds of discreditable things about the past career of the Tanganyikan politicians, although, if pressed, they become very vague about details. It is particularly interesting that this should be found here in Tanganyika, where independence came peacefully, and not in Kenya, where many present Ministers, including Kenyatta himself, were actually found guilty by British courts of participating in the Mau Mau conspiracy. In the same way, most of the British community condemns the "arse crawlers" who have taken political jobs with the black Government.

"Nobody wants to employ African reporters," said a British newspaperman, "but then nobody wants to employ Africans." A British pilot, raised in East Africa, was regretting having come back to work here: "It's changed a lot, and it's never good to come back to a place that has changed too much. And it's depressing to see the country going backwards. It's depressing to see six Africans doing the job that was being done by one European." He does not think that Africans will ever make sure pilots, as, so he says, they do not know how to keep calm in time of crisis. An engineer who is building a cement works in Dar es Salaam said, "Trying to build a cement works here is like farting against thunder. We've been four months already, and just about all we've got done is a hole in the ground . . . I'm here as long as Nyerere's here, and as soon as he goes you won't see me for for a cloud of dust."

Some of the former colonial officers who have been taken on by the new Government have settled in well, but complain, rightly or wrongly, of being saddled with too much work. Here is one man, half lightheartedly, speaking over the phone to a friend: "I've just spent all Saturday and Sunday and up to eight at night translating this speech from English into Swahili. I haven't had the time yet to make the application for the scholarships to England and if they're not in within a week nobody will go. I rather hope that happens. It's the only way this Government will learn, if I have to say that the Minister's brother can't go to England because I was doing three jobs at once. 'Drop all the other work,' he says. How can I? This Government's like an army that has half its men killed before it changes the training program. I haven't had time to write to my family for three weeks. I haven't been able to renew my gun license or my car license. If I'm arrested I'll say I'm building a nation."

The phone rang again. The civil servant winced, picked up the receiver and listened, winced again, and started talking. He was organizing the departure for Britain of a group of Tanganyikans with special scholarships in their trades or professions. The man on the other end of the line was worried about a clause in his contract which committed him to returning to Tanganyika after the expiry of the scholarship. The civil servant was trying to persuade him to sign: "Listen, Bwana, everyone has to sign that form or they can't go. The reason you have to sign it is that many people have behaved disgracefully in the past by going to England for two years, eating their heads off and then, instead of coming back to their jobs here, going off to run the Tokyo Fire Brigade or something . . . Of course you don't like signing it . . . Listen, Bwana, I went to hospital for an operation a few years ago and I had to sign a form beforehand saying that if I died it was all my own responsibility. I didn't like signing that either. No, of course you're not going to be dismissed. You're being promoted. You've been chosen to go to England out of millions of people. You've just got butterflies in the stomach like you do before a football match. Go on, Bwana, and sign." He put the phone down and grinned. "It's a funny job we have," he said. He evidently loves it, speaks fluent Swahili and gets on very well with his African assistant. This sort of man, who chose to serve in the colonies, has adapted better to independence, perhaps, than those who came to Africa by chance or just to make money. The second type, unfortunately, prevails now in Tanganyika and is responsible for part of the bad blood with the locals.

Overt proof of this bad blood came at the end of 1963, when the Tanganyikan Government took over the Dar es Salaam Club, which had been the main social center of English and other European residents. The confusion and rumor surrounding this takeover are all too representative of the distrust between the races in Tanganyika. At first I kept hearing the British version: "There were nearly a hundred British members, and most of the others were Europeans. The entrance fee was twenty-five pounds, and there was a long process of joining. However, there was no color bar in principle, and some Africans did join. But some of the politicians thought it was exclusive, so they put in nearly seventy applications at once. They were told the applications would have to go through the usual channels, whereupon they nationalized the club. Old members were told they would have to rejoin the club at an entrance fee of ten shillings. Most of them refused and went over to the Yacht Club or the Gymkhana Club. As a result the Dar Club is taking a loss, and some people fear that the Government will try to recoup this by nationalizing the two other clubs." That was a post office executive. Another Englishman said, "This used to be the posh club until they kicked us out. Yes, they told me I wasn't a member any more, and I've never got my twenty-five pounds back. There were seventy-eight British members of the club, but there was never a squeak from the British press." I asked a local journalist why this apparent injustice had gone unreported. Apparently the facts are not quite as the British tell them.

The club had been in the red for some years, but had come into sudden affluence by selling a plot of land at the back of the building. Moreover, it did discriminate in that applications by Africans got held up interminably in "the usual channels." There had been a move a few years back to speed up the entrance system and therefore make it possible for more Africans to join. But any change in the constitution required the approval of two thirds of the members. Since most of the members were abroad this meant a long postal vote to which many people did not reply. The Tanganyikan Government had simply lost patience.

The secretary of the club, Major Ernest Held, confirmed this: "There was nothing to stop colored people from joining, but the committee tended to be restrictive. A block of sixty-seven people was put up by the Minister of Foreign Affairs, Mr. Kambona. The committee, who couldn't see what was happening under their noses, turned it down. They said these people would have to put in their applications in the usual way. I told them there'd be trouble. This isn't an English Government, it's an African Government. The next day I was called over by the Government to discuss the sale of the club. I was told by the committee to give a selling price of £150,000, which was ludicrous. The Minister laughed, and the next day he said, 'Very well, we'll take the thing over for nothing.' They agreed to compensate members for their joining fees, but they haven't done so yet."

Major Held seemed to have had an intriguing time since the club was nationalized: "I couldn't take any more of this nonsense here. It was driving me crazy. There won't be any Europeans here in five or six months' time unless things change very drastically." The club is a Government hotel and its restaurant is patronized by most of the new black ruling class. There are still copies of *Country Life* in the lounge. The wooden airplane propeller still hangs on the wall of the bar; but the bar itself is empty. The guests on the veranda are mostly Africans who talk loudly, shout unclubland greetings from table to table, hold hands in the African fashion and tap their feet to the sway of High Life songs on the loudspeaker. Major Held surveys it all with mixed feelings. "I get on very well with the ministers here, but some of the lower types are terrible. We had a party of

Zanzibaris in who were eating with their fingers even though cutlery had been provided." But that same evening the spectacled, fanatic Zanzibar leader, Mr. Banga, was tucking into a three-course meal and wine with exquisite table manners.

Major Held is one of the wandering whites of Africa. He has been an engineer in South Africa, a farmer in Kenya, and a hotelier. Four years ago, he told me, he went back to his farm upon returning from a holiday to find the place stripped. "They even took the lavatory pans. I had a parquet floor. They took every tile of it up. I think it was the aftermath of the Mau Mau, the Land Freedom Army. So it was back to work as secretary of the Dar Club." With the nationalization of the club, Major Held, at sixty-three, thought it was time to move again. "I had thought of going to South Africa, but there are so many immigrants going there that at my age it would be hard to get a job. Besides, I think South Africa will be another Algeria, with sabotage and infiltration . . . The whole of Africa is going to suffer, and in my opinion it's all our faults. We haven't trained the Africans. We haven't given them a chance to progress. So in turn, they get cunning, or clever if you prefer, and learn the wrong way." Fate was kind to the wandering major. A few days before President Tubman of Liberia had been a guest at the Dar es Salaam Club. He liked the way it was organized, and called for Major Held and offered him the job of Controller of the President's Palace at Monrovia. "It's an opportunity I'm very proud of," Major Held told me. "Mr. Tubman is a splendid man."

The Europeans now mostly frequent the Yacht Club or the Gymkhana Club. Both are in fact, if not in principle, white clubs, and the conversation has the kind of banality that is found only in the colonies or ex-colonies. "We were talking about that English girl who got stabbed. They say it was her boy friend, a European, and there's no smoke without a fire . . . She wouldn't tell the police who had done it, so it must have been a European. If it had been one of them, she would have said." Other Europeans frequent the veranda bar of the New Africa Hotel, the social vortex of Dar es Salaam. Already the thought of it gives a twinge of nostalgia: the sound of the bicycle bell which the waiters ring when paging guests with messages; the habitual tropic smell of warm, corrupt fruit, and urine; the view past the cream-colored Luthern church and across the yacht-filled bay to the mango groves. A few tables away I noticed a tall, elderly Englishman with straw-colored hair and beard, a long, curved nose like a pirate's, Viking blue eyes and a pair of spectacles hung round his neck on a cord in the old Africa fashion. He turned out to be John Brown, a former agricultural officer who is living out his retirement on Sinda, a desert island seven miles south of Dar es Salaam.

A few days later we sailed in a friend's yacht to visit this very original hermit. Sinda is a coral island, and we swam across the reef to land. Just at that moment a nest of sea turtles hatched, and the youngsters, not two inches long, started their scramble towards the sea. This island of seventy-six acres was seldom even visited when Brown bought it in 1954, and it was not until 1961, after a bout of TB, that he moved in. He brought four servants with him from up-country—he does not approve of the coast Africans—and taught them first to swim and then to handle boats. They were such landlubbers that one of them tried to drink the sea water. The island was infested with snakes, mostly spitting cobras, but Brown poisoned the rats on which they fed, and the snakes swam off to other islands. At this time he lived in a *shamba* of bamboo and reed by the seashore. Since then he has built a fine house of cement with a corrugated iron roof. Inside is a screen decorated with a painted elephant, many carvings of lion and rhino, and a couple of ancient guns by the door. He has a radio and a mass of books: "People generally leave their paperbacks with me so that I have something to read. And when I've got through them it's time to start reading them over again." He was reading *Dr. Zhivago* at the time.

There are chickens, peacocks, three dogs, coconut palms and fruit trees on the island, but Brown's special pride is his massive bottle (or baobab) tree. "Have you seen my dancing girl?" he inquired, then hustled us out to look at the white patch on the grey of the bark which looked, if you stared hard enough, like a girl holding the side of her dress out for a polka. He sails over to Dar es Salaam once a week to buy provisions and hear the latest gossip. For a man who has chosen to live on his own on an island, he takes a remarkable interest in the world. A friend taunted him with having missed all the excitement of the mutiny in January, 1964. Brown denied this with indignation: "I didn't miss it. I was in Dar that day and I got stopped by the mutineers outside the barracks. Damned cheek. They made me miss my tide."

Friends sometimes visit Sinda for weekends. "You get woken up at half past six in the morning with a kick in the side and a bottle of beer," said one guest. "He's a marvelous sailor, that man. He would go out in anything in that boat and once took a load of furniture to the island in an eight-foot swell. I'd sail to England in it with him." In the Yacht Club at Dar es Salaam they call Brown the "Sultan of Sinda," a title he rather enjoys. When some fishermen were arrested there a few years ago, charged with dynamiting fish, the Court upheld Brown's claim that Sinda lies outside Tanganyikan jurisdiction. And Brown is not slow to exploit the fact. "I had another bash yesterday to get some duty-free hooch supplied to me, and Saccone and Speed say they are looking into it." The politics of the island are simple. "We have elections every day," Brown explains, "and I always elect myself." "One weekend we had a complete Cabinet here," added his friend, Fred, an American. "We had the dictator, John, the Financial Secretary, the Minister of War and the Attorney General—do you remember, that Dutch woman?" There is a notice PRIVATE LAND on this land where nobody comes, and much chaff about issuing visas.

The chaff conceals some real anxiety. The Sultan of Zanzibar was recently thrown out after a bloody revolution up north. The Sultan of Sinda has no intention of suffering the same fate: "Only the political situation is worrying, but I don't think they'll bother me, because I don't interfere in politics. The Zanzibaris won't land here. I won't let them . . . It's wonderful here. So peaceful. No bloody motor cars. And women are a nuisance too. If only you could get rid of them when you want and not when they want." We swam back to the yacht, leaving John Brown patrolling his little strip of sand with his dachshunds waddling along behind, and his bottle tree in the background. He is one white man in Africa to have solved the problem of staying on. He has, so to speak, cut a chunk off the continent and taken it out to sea. It is not, as somebody jested, "do-it-yourself apartheid." There are four Men Friday sharing the island with him, but he has cut himself off from the squabbles and jealousies of the mainland.

John Brown follows an honored tradition of white eccentricity in Tanganyika. It was from Dar es Salaam that Burton and Speke set off on their great expedition to Lake Tanganyika, inspired and refreshed for the miseries of the journey by their implacable jealousy and dislike of each other. The Germans, too, produced a Tanganyikan of genius, the soldier and partisan Paul von Lettow-Vorbeck, whose troops defied and infuriated the British throughout the entire First World War. With three thousand men he fought, confused, and pinned down a British force one hundred times as large. It is said that a hundred and thirty different Allied generals went into action against him, and that he caused the Allies sixty thousand casualties. He made a quinine substitute out of bark, made boots out of buffalo hide, and wove his own uniforms. He ate the same food as his native *askaris* and treated them with fairness. He freed his prisoners and once refused to shoot an opposing commander because he was too easy a target. Altogether he quite out-Badened Powell.

More recently there was John "Doc" Williamson, the geologist who had discovered the greatest diamond mine in the world in 1940. He had come to Tanganyika from Rhodesia in 1933, convinced that a seam of diamonds should, for geological reasons, be found just south of Lake Victoria. Nobody would believe him. One old acquaintance of Doc Williamson told me, "He was always broke and dirty and often drunk. Some people would kick him out into the gutter. Others generally gave him a few bob for a meal and a drink. He tried everywhere for the funds to prospect for these mines until one day he tried an Indian lawyer in Dar es Salaam (L. C. Chopra), who listened to him and decided it was worth lending him a couple of hundred pounds. Doc Williamson went off into the bush and got ill and was taken care of by an African woman. When he got better, she asked him why he had come there and he said for diamonds. 'Well, you've come to the right place,' she said. Apparently they knew about these stones, and soon he was a millionaire. And, you know, when he became rich he never forgot the people who knew him before.

He would try and break the people who had laughed at him. He'd find jobs for anybody who had befriended him." This slightly embroidered version of the career of the late Doc Williamson gives some idea of this legendary modern man.

"There's no fun here any more like there used to," said an Englishman in Dar es Salaam. "Too many bloody foreigners." He was not, I must hasten to add, referring to Tanganyikans. The whites in Africa never refer to the blacks as foreigners. Rather he meant that the British had lost their pride of place to the other white nationalities. Tanganyika was German before the First World War, and the Germans are active there now. When the TANU Party started its own newspaper this year the East Germans presented them with printing presses. The West Germans, not to be outdone, quickly sent a team of compositors and printers to help publish the newspaper. The East Germans, Russians and Chinese have scores of experts in Zanzibar, while on the mainland, which leans to the West, the West Germans and Israelis together equip and train the armed forces.

The "bloody foreigners" can generally be distinguished from the British by their clothes. They go in for blue or khaki shorts and loose shirts, with plenty of pockets, that hang outside the waist. Sandals and dark glasses are more popular than with the English. Naturally each nationality thinks it has some special knack at getting on with the Africans. There is much quiet boasting of a "more-interracial-than-thou" kind. The Americans, for instance, think that their own large colored community helps them to get on well with African Negroes. A plump, spectacled AID specialist from Columbia took this line as we talked in the one fashionable espresso bar of Dar es Salaam: "Americans coming here have the same problem as English people—dealing with Africans. You find some who react very negatively, a small minority who react very positively, and the majority, who mix a certain amount during office hours and keep apart in the evening. On the whole there are probably more Americans who mix easily because there are more who are used to mixing with Negroes. And British formality and stiffness is a big barrier. You find the same thing extending even to our State Department. If they ask Africans to their house, they ask them to dinner, whereas the African is used to dropping in on people. When they *do* drop in we're inclined to stare at them as though to say 'What are you doing here?' " Quite a number of Americans in Africa actually come from the South. Was there any resentment of this, I asked a Ford Foundation man, whose speech is larded with "caint's" and "you all's"? "They've never raised it," he said, and added, "After all, they've got South Africans here, even working in the police force. I've made many good African friends here. I take them sailing and swimming and they love it."

"The more sophisticated people are," said an Australian, "the more difficult it is for them to get on with Africans. That's why the Portuguese get on better than the English, the Italians better than the Czechs, the Chinese better than the Russians." Few of these people had ever seen a Russian in Africa, but claimed they were hopeless with the Africans. There is a story about a Russian delegation at Bamako, in the left-wing Republic of Mali, who find themselves obliged to share an hotel with a Chinese delegation. Both groups are refusing to speak to each other. The temperature is 110° in the shade, but both delegations wear suits and ties so as not to lose face. The air conditioning in the hotel has broken down, and everyone is afflicted with terrible thirst by lunchtime. But the tap water is riddled with dysentery germs, and the hotel has run out of tinned Evian water. The Russians, drenching their thick serge suits with sweat, drink glass after glass of claret . . .

Most Europeans in Tanganyika acknowledge the skill of the Israelis at working with, and helping, the Tanganyikans. Of course, in principle the Israelis are Asians rather than Europeans, but the Africans themselves do not make this distinction. Clearly the Israelis are not brown like the Indians; clearer still, they are not Arabs. The Africans, therefore, sensibly call them Europeans. Like most newcomers to Africa, I was surprised at the extensive presence and influence of tiny Israel. In most independent countries south of the Sahara one finds Israeli experts on agriculture, hydrology, medicine, soil preservation and youth movements. Hundreds of Africans go on courses to Haifa and Tel Aviv. Professional anti-Semites, who are common among the whites in Africa, explain this simply as Jewish economic imperialism. Certainly many Israeli firms find welcome markets in Africa. There may be also a political move to win black African friends as a balance to the North African Arabs. But anyone who has met Israelis working in Africa—or for that matter in Israel—would be wrong to discount their strong and genuine idealism. The Israelis are proud of having made their own poor country into a great economic power. They are eager to give the benefit of their experience to the Africans. At a deeper level they are anxious to see the Negro race prove itself equal to any other. The Jews know all there is to know of the horrors of racial prejudice.

A British architect, in crisp white shirt and stock, was complaining about the state of the building industry: "I tell them they can't put a second floor of the kind they want on top of this first floor. They insist. So I say, 'Very well, if that's how you want it. But it won't last more than a few years.' There's one building starting to crack already, I'm delighted to see." Bearing in mind this view of Africans as builders, I went to talk with the Israelis who are constructing the eleven-story Kilimanjaro Hotel for the Tanganyikan Government. The three men, Chaim Presente, site engineer, Amram Marteffy, of the Administrative Department, and Zui Heimlich, the superintendent, are employed by Solel Boneh, the construction company of the Israeli trade unions. All these men have the experience of building in different countries, but their view of African abilities is quite different from that of the British. They began the hotel in September, 1963. It was due to be completed two years later, and construction was, if anything, ahead of schedule. All the skilled and unskilled workers on the site are

Africans. "We gave a three-month course to anyone who wanted it in reading drawings, measurements and so on," said Mr. Presente. "About sixteen men attended—skilled laborers—and now they are about as good as we could get anywhere. At first they had to be supervised in everything. Now the steel fixers do everything independently. Carpenters? We have some who can work independently and others who have to be helped sometimes. Most of them can read plans. Also there was a difficulty in that we introduced new methods like coffers and girders." "When we first came here," said Mr. Heimlich, who came here himself ten months ago and had taught himself English during that period, "they weren't very advanced. Now they are about at the level of Europe."

The hotel when completed will have eleven stories, a swimming pool, and a casino, which is decorously referred to in brochures and the local press as the Function Room. The Tanganyikan Government has given another Israeli firm the concession to operate the hotel. They are now looking for twelve senior African operators to study the trade for a year in Israel. It can be seen that Israeli help works both ways. For instance, the plywood used in the coffers of the Kilimanjaro Hotel comes from the Afikim *kibbutz* near the Sea of Galilee. The Afikim plywood factory buys much of its timber from Tanganyika and other African countries. The fact that Israel profits from giving aid should not obscure the fact that they give the kind of aid—in practical training—that Africa most needs.

"We think some of the English here are very Poonah, very stuck-up," said one of these Israelis. "They seem to look down on Africans. We always like to show the Africans how to work by doing it ourselves, not just by telling them how. We treat them as equals, although, of course, we also have to remind them that we're the bosses at work." Since I am ignorant of the techniques of the building industry, it is impossible to judge by results how well these men have worked—although the fact that the hotel was half built must speak for itself. It was possible to see that the African workers were getting on with their work with quiet efficiency and a minimum of puzzled complaints. Many Europeans complain that Africans are lazy and dull and slow to learn. This may depend very much on the way they are treated.

These Israeli engineers worked hard, sometimes for eighteen hours at a stretch. But from the way they talked it was clear that they liked Tanganyika. They were amused when I asked if the Israeli community in Dar es Salaam had a club. "That's the first thing the English want, a club. We're not the type for clubs. In our spare time we pay social visits and go to the cinema. We don't play cards and we don't drink so much." He tactfully did not say than whom they drank less. If these remarks sound a little priggish in print, this is a false impression. The Israelis I met here and elsewhere in Africa (as indeed those I have met in Israel) seemed to react to the continent with considerable gusto and none of those fits of melancholy that beset the northern Europeans.

The following day I visited Noah Cohen, one of the Israeli advisors to COSATA, the newly formed Co-operative Supply Association of Tanganyika Limited. Now, Tanganyika is the most co-operatively minded State in Africa, and Dar es Salaam is the Pan-African Co-operative Headquarters. Even before the war the British encouraged co-operative farming of cotton and coffee. Today one-third of all exports come from co-operative enterprises. But until two years ago there was no retail co-operative organization, and almost all the retail trade was run by Asians or Arabs. In July, 1962, the Israeli Co-operative took a 20 per cent share in COSATA, which now has twenty-three stores and a staff of two hundred and fifty. "The business is important," says Mr. Cohen, "but not as important as the training. COSATA is a school. All the workers have had to take intensive courses and examinations, without compromise"—this is a favorite Cohen phrase. "We teach the management staff the principles of the co-operative movement, knowledge of goods—for instance, which are the more caloric foodstuffs—planning, hygiene and cleanliness. We insist that people should be good in mathematics. We don't allow any compromise in this field." The Israelis have tried to instill a feeling for public relations: "The Government has encouraged its employees to use COSATA, and the last supermarket was opened by six Ministers. There are COSATA songs which women sing outside the shops on patriotic occasions."

COSATA has tried to introduce a change in shopping psychology. "In all other shops you have to bargain,"

Cohen explained; "you can cut the price down by half. But at COSATA you have fixed prices and a very low margin of profit. We are never satisfied with our prices. We continually check with other stalls to see that we are selling at the market price, or less." One of the problems of COSATA concerns the psychology of salesmanship. The Israelis, or at any rate the Jews of the Diaspora, are world renowned for their special commercial flair. The Africans have never shown much interest. All over the continent it is the Arabs, Syrians, Indians, Greeks and Portuguese who keep the small shops. One Israeli in Tanganyika said, "If you go into a shop belonging to an Indian he comes forward, smiles and tries to sell you something. An African is inclined just to stand there." Although COSATA was intended just for Africans, there are numerous Asians among the staff, thanks to their knowledge of skills like bookkeeping and shorthand and typing.

Inevitably the Israeli interest in COSATA has aroused hostility from some other Europeans. "They run everything here," an Englishman complained. "You see Israeli goods in all the shops—Israeli soap, Israeli clothes. That's what they want here—a market for their goods." This accusation is wildly exaggerated. Even in COSATA shops there is only a small range of Israeli goods: refrigerators, air conditioners, and motor accessories. Most European countries share the foodstuff trade, while the Japanese—as throughout Africa—have cornered the market in dresses decorated with the face of the local political leader.

I was not surprised to hear that Cohen greatly enjoyed his stay in Tanganyika: "It's good soil here, and I wish we in Israel had that water. I blame Moses sometimes that he came where he did and not to Africa."

As a matter of fact, the Jews very nearly did come to East Africa. This was not the plan of Moses but of the British Government, which in 1903 offered the Kenya Highlands as a Jewish national home. If the Zionists had accepted this idea, a Jewish State might have been formed long before the Nazi persecution and enabled a much larger Israel to be formed. However, the Jews might have found the Kikuyu just as uncomfortable neighbors as the Arabs.

Mr. Cohen likes the Africans: "We are open people. We speak our mind. But when necessary we can be tough, and they respect you for this." In Dar es Salaam, Mr. Cohen acquired a distinction rare, if not unique, among his fellow countrymen: "I made history, you know. I lectured in a mosque. The Ismaili community came to me and asked if I would talk to them about productivity. So I talked to two hundred of them in their mosque."

I said at the beginning of this chapter that Tanganyika served as a bogy country to the whites of Kenya. The whites in Tanganyika have their own little bogy island of Zanzibar twenty miles to the north. I took the plane there armed with a pass signed by the Chief Immigration Officer of the United Republic of Tanganyika and Zanzibar. After a long delay at Zanzibar airport they said this was not valid. From whom, then, should I get an entry permit? "From the Foreign Office of Zanzibar," said the immigration policeman. "But you haven't got a Foreign Office," I protested. He merely shrugged and grinned. Expelled on the same plane by which I had come, I sat on the veranda beside the Anna Pauker-like customs girl, and a sentry admiring the flower held in his toes.

There are all sorts of rumors the Tanganyika whites tell of Zanzibar or its sister island of Pemba. Anyone (in Pemba) involved in a motor accident, however badly hurt, is immediately tied to a tree and publicly flogged . . . One European is expelled (from Zanzibar) every day, on principle . . . During the revolution in Zanzibar the British people gathered at the English Club and passed the time playing Monopoly. As the atrocities outside grew more bloody and the lips inside grew more stiff, the players made an amusing change in the game. Names like Whitechapel and Bond Street and Park Lane were changed to Revolutionary H.Q. and Concentration Camp and Sultan's Palace. It was an extremely impressive gesture, everybody agrees. I wonder if anyone was really impressed by it except the English themselves.

The rumors about Zanzibar may or may not be true. They serve as a soothing therapy to the whites. The distress of a neighbor adds excitement and heroism to one's own life. It feeds the suspicion that everyone (that is, the blacks) are hostile—without the reality of danger.

After Kenya and Tanganyika, the impressions one gets of Uganda are peaceful and green. Here the visitor, even the white visitor, is made to feel at ease. The three main towns—Entebbe, Kampala and Jinja—ring the north-western shore of Lake Victoria bask all the year round at a temperature in the seventies. Politically, too, the temperature stays in the 70s. The United People's Congress stands solid behind Dr. Milton Obote, a compromiser and one of the shrewdest politicians in Africa. Apart from some tribal troubles along the Sudanese and Congo borders, scarcely a breath of passion now affects Ugandan politics, except when yet another Opposition leader gets bored and decides to join the UPC.

It is little more than a century since Burton and Speke set out to find the source of the White Nile. When Burton, wrongly, claimed to have found it in Lake Tanganyika, and Speke, rightly, in Lake Victoria, the two men clashed in a famous Victorian quarrel. Ironically, there is now a Burton Street in Kampala, close to the river he never believed was the Nile source. Even more ironically, Speke Street has been changed to Kampala Street and the great discoverer is remembered more by the Speke Hotel and the Maison Speke Limited, Ladies and Gents Hair Stylists. A dam for a hydroelectric power station has flooded out the Ripon Falls that Speke discovered, incidentally converting the source of the Nile once more into a political controversy. When the Israeli Government offered aid in the form of hydroelectric experts, the Uganda Government suspected some kind of plot against Egypt. So did the

Egyptians, who now have two men posted at Jinja to inspect the instruments on the dam each morning to make sure that enough water is flowing down into Egypt. The Europeans at Jinja have lesser worries: "Jinja has the distinction," said a Scottish agricultural engineer, "of being the one place where hippopotamuses walk across the golf course and you may have to hole out of one of their footprints. There's one coffee grower here who, for a bet, will stick a postage stamp on a hippo's backside."

During Uganda's years as a protectorate, the whites and blacks had lived together in peace and harmony. Independence came without bloodshed or ill will. The country is rich enough from coffee and cotton to earn one of the few favorable balance-of-payments records in Africa. Here, if anywhere, there is reason to expect racial harmony. Yet, the remaining British are almost as sour and carping as their counterparts in Tanganyika. Here again one meets men in colonial white shirts and shorts, with views to match. Their manners are atrocious. For instance, an Englishman lunching in Jinja, within easy hearing of Africans at the next table, loudly proclaimed: "The local nig-nogs call Jinja the Detroit of East Africa. Bah!" Another man, hearing of the Peace Corps's arrival, made the comment: "Poor buggers. We had some people like that before, and after two years only one per cent of them were impressed by the Africans. And they were the sort who were impressed by the golliwog on the Robertson's jam jar when they were children." Here was another Englishman on the Peace

Corps: "I hope they're not like that bloody lot we sent out (Teachers for East Africa)—scruffy, bearded fellows. There was one of them sitting next to me in the theater at Kampala, you know, when they did that play, and he was in a stained shirt and very short shorts, and, mind you, I've seen mechanics wearing cleaner shorts than that. He stank. I wish some of them had come over here to the Jinja Yacht Club. We've got the whole lake to wash them in, even if we had to tow them round, sprinkling washing powder on them all the way." The Teachers for East Africa provoked another Englishman into still greater fury: "D'yer know the City Bar? There was a European girl came in there this evening in a sari. She was with a man in a big beard and two Africans—and her feet were bare, she had no shoes, oh dear, oh dear." The same man mourned: "Kenya's a white man's country. But this is black man's country." The unease of the British, and their resulting boorishness, is widely blamed on what is always called the Tank Hill Affair. It is a curious story and worth retelling in detail.

Among the party-going British there had always been a small number of single young men and bachelor girls who found themselves constantly asked out by married friends. In order to repay this hospitality, they had got into the habit of clubbing together in December each year to hold a giant party for all their hosts of the previous twelve months. These parties were usually held somewhere in Tank Hill, the most fashionable of the seven hills on which Kampala is built. It had always been the tradition to provide some comic theme for the party;

in 1962, for instance, it had been called a "sludge-drinking" party.

The organizers of the party in 1963 were a girl representative of the Save the Children Fund in Uganda and six young men—the town engineer of Mengo, an electrical engineer with the Uganda Electricity Board, an insurance branch manager, a tea taster, and two coffee executives. Noticing that the party was going to coincide with Kenya's independence day on December 12th, they decided to make this year's theme "the laying down of the white man's burden." The facetious invitations to 200—apparently all white—guests asked for reply by bearer carrying cleft stick, and the humor was evidently on this level. (The hostess at least appeared at the party in African national dress.) Some of the guests said afterwards that the whole thing was a satire on imperialism but, to judge by the British people I met in Uganda, it is a fair guess that African self-rule came in for equal mockery. At any rate, the 200 reckoned it a successful party and, by dawn on December 13th, thought it was all over, barring the hangovers.

The Government just at this time had run into difficulties. The price of coffee had had to be lowered, which irritated the farmers. Meanwhile, the proposed law to bring missionary schools into the state education system had aroused great protest from the Roman Catholics, who make up a third of the population. There is some reason to think that the Government wanted to find a scapegoat to divert public resentment away from itself. If so, they had not far to look.

At first a mere murmur warned of the coming hurricane. A short inside story in the *Uganda Argus* of December 18 reported that "police visited the houses of seven young Europeans, six men and one woman on Monday and took away documents and tape recordings relating to a party held in a house on Tank Hill on Thursday evening." There was a brief statement to this effect from Gerald Murphy, senior assistant commissioner, CID. The following evening, December 19th, a UPC youth wing leader, Ally Mukalazi, gave the public its first inkling of what had happened. Denouncing the party as "subversive" he claimed that "an insult to Kenya is indeed an insult to Uganda . . . Other Europeans living in Uganda who play with our sovereignty and do not recognize the African personality will be dealt with strongly."

The following day, December 20th, Dr. Obote himself raised the matter in Parliament and produced what he called the evidence. There was a card in a cleft stick, a wooden imitation of a shrunken skull, and worst of all, the text of a song, part of which he read to the House: "*Uhuru, uhuru, uhuru, uhuru* is good enough for me," went to refrain. A typical verse ran: ". . . we are bound to make a few mistakes/We have not got the brains/And also it's undignified/For man to clear out drains." This silly document had been found among the private papers of one of the men who had been searched. The police claimed that the song had been sung at the party. The accused man replied, apparently truthfully, that he had heard it sung by an American entertainer in a

Nairobi night club several years earlier, but had not looked at the songsheet since.

When Obote had finished, other M.P.s pressed home their indignation. One described how a woman at the party was made to wear a *busuti*, a rope was tied round her neck and she was pulled here and there: "This meant that when an African becomes independent, that is how he treats a woman." Claiming that these people were part of the Ku Klux Klan which had murdered President Kennedy, he called for a charge of high treason against everyone who had attended the party. "These people in Britain wanted to keep Britain white," said Y. M. Chemonges, and, adding, "we should keep ourselves black." Another M.P. wanted all civil servants involved with the party to be "put in the prison, in the dark rooms for a hundred years." Still another asked for the closing of Entebbe airport, and then "that we try these people and then flog them." Yet another wanted a "bill introduced that would forbid Europeans attending meetings or assemblies in Uganda because it was at these meetings that they planned such activities." Closing this distasteful discussion on a slightly more moderate note, Dr. Obote said the organizers had invited 200 friends and yet none of them was an African. He hoped that an African "will not be number 201 on anybody else's friendship list."

The incident was by no means closed. Because it was falsely rumored that the *Uganda Argus* staff had been at the party, the manager was kidnapped by toughs on December 21st and made to carry a bunch of bananas on his head. On December 22nd, an unknown group burned down the house where the party had been held, even although the owner himself had been absent. A dog was burned to death—the only casualty in this tragi-comic affair. Just before Christmas, six of the alleged organizers were deported to England. Although many, if not most African politicians, deprecated the violent language used by extremists, the affair left a nasty taste in everybody's mouth. It was yet another catastrophe caused by the Englishman's lack of a sense of humor.

"Things were bad for six months after the Tank Hill affair," said an Englishman in Kampala, and even now the atmosphere is unhappy. The British and Ugandans seem constrained when they meet at social gatherings. The normally middle-road government suffers from bouts of xenophobia and spy mania. There are threats against the harmless *Uganda Argus;* in December radio telephones and transmitters were withdrawn from British tea planters in West Uganda in case they should try to signal fellow whites in Tshombe's Congo. The unpleasantness between the races is all the more sad, so wiser Ugandans say, because it never existed before independence. It is too easy to blame just the Tank Hill affair.

The British in Uganda seem particularly prone to boredom. What syphilis does for the white man's sex-life in Africa, bilharziasis does for his social life. The malignant snail which has come up the Nile to infest Lake Victoria makes swimming suicidally dangerous. Most British will not even sail or fish for fear of catching the disease from the spray. There is golf, of course, and the chance for spending a weekend at one of the game reserves to the west. But most of the Englishmen in Kampala pass their leisure at billiards in the City Bar or at drinking elsewhere. It is a place full of sad, solitary men on bar stools: "I'm one of those people the Labor Government doesn't like: I've got a private income. I retired in 1962 from East Africa and went back to the U.K. and got terribly bored. I couldn't stand it, by Jove. So I signed on for three years more—my retirement comes up soon. I'm going to spend one year at Malindi (on the Kenya coast)—I've always wanted to have a go at the marlin—one year in Salisbury, and one year in Natal. And I've got a bit of property in the Bahamas so I want to spend some time there, and then I want to go to New Guinea. I'm determined to see the Birds of Paradise before I die."

The British concentrate in the Kampala Club, which is not to be confused with the Uganda Club. The Uganda Club is patronized by many Ugandans, as well as foreigners. The Kampala Club is multiracial, too, said one member, but he said it with a smile. "The Africans are free to join," he went on, "but they don't want to come." One cannot altogether blame them. The club and it members belong to some second-rate novel about the thirties by Somerset Maugham. In the "Men Only" bar on a Saturday lunchtime, the members gather in shirts and shorts or flannel trousers to bemoan the pace of Africanization. Their wives sit in the bamboo chairs on the veranda talking of servants. Most of them are harmless and free from malice; but the tone of the club rings strange in independent Africa. It is said that Lord Caradon (former Sir Hugh Foot) would not visit the club when he came to Kampala. Nor, for that matter, will the American residents. "They say it's a last vestige of imperialism," said a member, "though perhaps they may be pulling our legs."

Probably the Americans were quite serious. In contrast to most of the British, they take great pains to avoid giving offense to local sentiment. When talking, for instance, to Moses L. Perry, organizing secretary of the Y.M.C.A. in Jinja, I chanced to refer to the Royal Government, meaning the Royal Buganda Government which controls a quarter of the country. "You mustn't talk about royalists now," said Perry in a shocked voice. He is a Negro from Florida and has been in Uganda two years helping to start a Y.M.C.A. club. Most of the members are Asians rather than Africans because the premises lie in the Asian commercial district. But Perry is proud of their achievements: "Our work has been very well supported. We're very proud of that. There was a certain amount of opposition from the Hindus—'Why do you call yourselves a Christian organization?' —but we said we weren't proselytizing, even though we're a Christian organization."

White racists in Africa frequently claim that American Negroes who visit the continent are appalled by the backwardness and savagery they see. My experience indicates otherwise. I have met colored Americans, even in the Congo, who felt at home simply because of the friendly, welcoming people they met. They often found Africa, and even the Congo, less tense than their home states in America. If the elite in independent African countries are far less sophisticated than quite ordinary colored Americans, they have the compensating advantage of confidence. Often Africans find it hard to identify Negroes with the United States.

In Kampala I met Phelon De Lafayette Peters, a light-skinned Negro from Los Angeles who was lecturing throughout eastern Africa on the American space program. What did they think about his being colored, I asked. "Often they didn't believe it," Peters replied. "They're very dark-skinned and I'm very light-skinned. And I had to tell them I was." He had enjoyed his series of talks for the U.S.I.S. in Ethiopia, Somalia, and Uganda: "The sophisticated view it as part and parcel of an advancing society. The less sophisticated view it as part and parcel of witchcraft and black magic . . . People outside America are much more concerned with the space race . . . They're satisfied that I've given them information they've not had before and the fact that I've had contact with spacemen gives me a certain kudos." The questions put to him were much the same as he got when lecturing in the northeast United States—principally concerning what *they* would have to do to qualify as an astronaut.

At the time I was in Uganda, the Americans were having their first real taste of unpopularity. The Ugandans, like most Africans, had interpreted the relief of Stanleyville as white imperialism. Because of this the

Americans, who had never colonized so much as an acre in Africa, assumed all the odium of a colonial power. There were demonstrations, threats and harsh speeches —to the scarcely concealed joy of the British. The Americans viewed their unpopularity with concern. "For about a week they just didn't want to listen," said a U.S. official in Kampala; "there were really bad relations between Africans and Americans. They would stay away from parties, for instance. There was one young UPC youth group extremist who stood up and told the crowd: 'Let's grab arms and march on the Congo, killing all the Americans on the way.' Somehow the New York *Times* got hold of this and printed it and, as a result, about two hundred tourists stayed away . . . We don't like being called bastards any more than anyone. Some Africans think they can get up and call us bastards in public and go on being friendly in private. We don't think that way. In the United States people aren't allowed to demonstrate within two hundred yards of an embassy—in fact, a couple of blocks. I think we're going to demand the same here."

These remarks show the difference between the British and American attitudes in Africa. The Americans are more disposed to be friendly, sympathetic and interested. As a consequence, they are more quick to take offense when their friendship is shunned. The British are too often supercilious, standoffish, and bored. But five hundred years of imperialism have taught them not to be too perturbed by unpopularity.

Ethiopia

IN 1520 a Portuguese priest made his way into Ethiopia and was received by the people with kindness. The Emperor asked for his help and advice on government, agriculture and architecture, behaving, indeed, as a perfect host, except for refusing to let the European go home. The unfortunate priest was obliged to stay six years before getting permission to voyage back.

In 1964 a group of British administrators and technicians started a TV station in Addis Ababa for the Ministry of Information. The cameras were old-fashioned and there was no Ethiopian with the knowledge to use them. Much of the staff had been given their jobs through personal influence; there were less than a thousand TV sets in the whole empire. But the station caught the imagination of Emperor Haile Selassie, who soon started to call in each day, even although this meant a climb of three stories to the studio in the top of the unfinished City Hall. And so it came about that when the station was operating and the British experts were ready to go home, the Emperor was reluctant to let them go. He did not detain them or even expressly prevent them getting their exit visas. But he let it be known, in the pleasantest manner imaginable, that they must stay.

The two incidents, so far apart in time, sum up the experience of the white man in Ethiopia. For hundreds of years travelers have been horrified, enchanted, and amazed by the people of this truly fantastic kingdom. The Ethiopians are compounded of paradox. They were Christians before the English but nine out of ten of them still cannot read. They are black but often call themselves white, and the whites call themselves pink. They never discovered the wheel but are some of the finest pilots in the world. They support over a hundred thousand priests and some twenty thousand prostitutes. They have fewer children at school than almost any other country in Africa, but some of the cleverest college graduates. They are among the most kind, witty and courteous hosts in the world, but only two score years ago still castrated their prisoners. Their aristocrats are the most urbane since the days of Louis XIV—and their favorite food is newly killed raw beef doused in pimento sauce, washed down with a beaker of mead. They are somewhere between the Old Testament and the New Deal.

When you fly to Ethiopia and the captain announces, "We are now at an altitude of eleven thousand feet," it is disturbing to look out of the window and find the plane winging low over Addis Ababa. Most of Ethiopia lies more than a mile and a half high and this fact explains its three thousand years of independence. Range after range of craggy mountains have made it a fortress in eastern Africa. When the Arabs, Sudanese and Turks tried to take it by storm, their camels died of cold and their warriors lost heart in the thin, rainy atmosphere. The country remains remote even in our jet age. At least one ancient city had to be struck from the itinerary of the British queen this year because her plane might have been in danger from landing at too great a height.

In other African countries the invaders tried to convert the natives to Christianity. In Ethiopia the natives tried to convert their Moslem invaders. Having accepted Christianity in the fourth century from two very persuasive castaways, the Ethiopians have remained true to their ritual and to their very distinctive interpretation of the Athanasian creed. The nation that once waged war because an Italian artist depicted the Christ child on the left instead of the right arm of the Virgin Mary must be one of the most devout in Christendom; it used to be said that there was one priest for every five Ethiopians.

The long church services take one back almost to St. Paul's age. The priests and deacons, in bare feet but gold and white turbans and robes, proceed round and about the Host—three men to hold up the candles, two to hold up the Holy Book for the priest to read, four to open and shut the curtains which hide certain mysteries from the congregation, one—in a modern cathedral—to move the microphone, others to sprinkle holy water upon the elbows and faces of the communicants, more to hold out a hand for the ritual kiss. Birds flutter in the rafters but nothing mars the ritual of the church, which is also the ceremonial myth of the nation. The men, to the left, in jodhpurs and flowing burnous, lean during the service on shepherds' crooks. The women stand on the right; and when the time comes to crouch in prayer they envelop themselves in long muslin shawls, like a chorus of mourners in some Greek tragedy.

Ethiopia lured and intrigued Europeans even before they quite knew where it was. Legends of Prester John and the Queen of Sheba up in the "mountains of the moon" appealed especially to literary gentlemen from Herodotus to Dr. Johnson. Indeed when James Bruce, the Scottish explorer who reached the source of the Blue Nile in 1770, told of his experiences in a book, Dr. Johnson was one of the many pundits who accused him of inaccuracy. The stories Bruce told of Ethiopian life were bound to deflate the romantic fantasies: torture, castration, mass murder were commonplace in this dark era of Ethiopian history. And Bruce's enemies were particularly horrified by his account of how Ethiopians, when hungry, would cut steaks from a live bull and immediately eat the raw, quivering flesh. The cruelty which appalled Bruce rather attracted Richard Burton, who visited Harar, the slaving city, some eighty years later. The public flogging of women seems particularly to have intrigued this demonic and brutal scholar. Another misfit, the French poet, Rimbaud, came to live in the same city of Harar later in the century.

It was largely the British who opened Ethiopia to the world during the nineteenth century. Various religious societies sent missionaries—often Germans—to preach and convert; the Queen appointed consuls at the court of the Emperor Theodore to win the support of this Christian power behind the Ottoman Empire. It was one of these consuls—Captain Charles Cameron—who was the cause of Ethiopia's first clash with a European power. Emperor Theodore, a neurotic if ever there was one, took offense when the British Foreign Office failed to reply to his letter of greeting. He imprisoned and tortured Cameron, then chained up most of the foreign community, including three more British diplomats who had been sent to get Cameron's release. For months and then years, the little group of white prisoners accompanied Theodore's mobile court on bloody campaigns throughout Ethiopia. He could be kind or threatening, maudlin or furious, just as the day's mood took him. At last the British lost patience.

The relief of the Stanleyville hostages in 1964 needed only a few planeloads of paratroopers. The British expedition of 1868 did not even arrive at the borders of Ethiopia until more than four years after Cameron's arrest. When it did arrive, it arrived in style: thirty-two thousand men, fifty-five thousand animals, including elephants, heavy mountain artillery, and the equipment for a railway. The campaign ended at Magdala, the mountain fortress where Theodore, his army, and his hostages had taken refuge. The Ethiopians came out to give battle, were shot down in droves and defeated. The hostages were released and Theodore shot himself. Their mission done, the British then marched back to the coast leaving Ethiopia to its independence. As a result, the modern Ethiopians bear no grudge against the British invaders. Indeed some of their primitive paintings of the events, showing Theodore's suicide in front of his conqueror, General Napier, show the Englishman the more regal of the two. Characteristically, the artists show Napier dark-skinned like an Indian, while Theodore is white.

The brief war bettered rather than spoiled Anglo-Ethiopian friendship. It was mostly British people who encouraged and helped Emperor Menelik in his modernizing work at the turn of the century. The putting down of slavery, the reform of taxation, and the bringing to heel of the feudal nobility were accomplished with British help and prodding. The Emperor would often consult the British consul even before his own ministers. There was a brief change in this policy during the First World War when the young Emperor Lij Jasu became influenced by the Germans. But after his deposition because of insanity, the young Ras Makonnen—later Haile Selassie I—returned to his old friendship with the Western Allies. Having been brought up in a French school, he particularly favored the French, Belgians and Swiss who provided, respectively, Ethiopia's railway, air force, and forestry service. By the time of the Emperor's coronation in 1930, all kinds of Europeans were employed throughout Ethiopia. Many White Russians had settled in Addis Ababa, whose thin phantasmagoric atmosphere encouraged their wild dreams of return. The Swedes, as fellow monarchists, gave Haile Selassie tips on Imperial etiquette.

Most European powers were prepared to lend Ethiopia help and advice. Only the Italians dreamed of making her subject. As early as 1887 an Italian army had tried to invade Ethiopia from the coastal colony of Eritrea. Barefoot Ethiopian warriors trapped the Italian army in the mountains and killed most of their men. Italian public opinion was to be shamed by this setback from savage Africans; the humiliation was made even more bitter to this nation so proud of its sexual virility because it was rumored about that the Ethiopian troops had mutilated the bodies of killed and captured Italians. The resentment lingered on into the twentieth century and the era of Mussolini. The "civilizing mission" in Ethiopia lasted from 1935 to 1941. But Mussolini's boasts made very little impression upon the country. Ethiopia may have been occupied, but she was no more colonized than was Poland by the Germans during the recent war, or Italy by the Americans. The invaders, long the best civil engineers in Europe, built a series of winding, expensive roads through the mountains. They laid out some attractive towns and erected handsome public buildings. They introduced the Italian language which the Ethiopians found easy to learn, so that even today in remote villages, where no Italians have been for a score of years, the urchins will still greet visiting Europeans with "*giorno signore*."

The need for living space had been one of the Duce's excuses for the invasion. Accordingly, many peasants and poor town dwellers were encouraged to settle in Ethiopia as farmers, tradesmen and artisans. They settled in well. The Blackshirt political officers tried to prevent racial mixing and encouraged the settlers to look down on the natives. But this kind of thinking did not come easily to the ordinary Italians who soon became friendly with the lighthearted Ethiopians. Hostility between the two peoples remained political rather than personal. The Blackshirts shot thousands of educated Ethiopians in reprisals against the partisans, but the Ethiopians did not take their revenge against ordinary Italians after the British liberation of 1941. The Addis Ababa crowd that ululated a greeting to Haile Selassie when he rode home, treated the former enemy with courtesy. Indeed, it was the British, and not the Ethiopians, who ordered all the Italians to be expelled to camps in Aden or Kenya. Many thousands of Italians managed to stay on in their adopted country by hiding out with Ethiopian friends. After the war, still more of them came back and they are now by far the largest foreign community in the country, and by far the most popular with the Ethiopians.

Occasionally Ethiopians profess to regret that the Italians did not stay longer. "All the good roads, all the good buildings were built by the Italians," said one morose intellectual. "Even countries like Kenya and Tanganyika are more advanced than us because they were colonies." But 3,000 years of freedom have given the Ethiopians something more precious than tarmac roads. Almost alone among African nations, they have pride and self-confidence. "An inferiority complex is the very last thing these people have," said a European diplomat in Addis Ababa. The Ethiopians, who claim to spring from a one-night affair between Solomon and the Queen of Sheba, regard more recent people with polite disdain. With their lean, handsome, rather Arabic faces, they tend to look down on the Bantu or Negro people in Central and West Africa.

Circumstances have combined to give Ethiopia great importance in Africa. Politically, it is midway between left-wing Ghana and the neocolonized countries. Racially, it is midway between the Bantu and the Arabs. Physically, it is a junction for air traffic and conferences. With a population of over twenty million it is stronger in numbers than any other African nation, bar Egypt and Nigeria; partly because of this it supports an effective army which served the United Nations with valor in Korea and the Congo. Above all, it appears to be stable. Bandits sometimes loot lonely motorists but there is no sign of civil disturbances—no riots, no stoning of embassies, no murder of missionaries. For all its poverty, Ethiopia has stuck to conservative policies in finance. She keeps her promises and pays her debts, which has proved an inducement to foreign investors. "If I was in London and was thinking where I would put my East African man," said a British trader, "I'd say Addis Ababa. It's a good listening post. People come here from all over Africa—foreign ministers, buyers, conference delegates. You get to know what's going on."

The Emperor welcomes this international traffic. He built a huge conference hall and offered it to the United Nations. As a result, both the Economic Commission for Africa and the Organization for African Unity have their headquarters in Addis Ababa. "On No Account Are Animal Skins Allowed To Be Taken Out Of Ethiopia" say the placards inside Africa Hall. But the innumerable delegates to the endless succession of conferences bring plenty of money into the country, regardless of what they take out. The Ethiopians treat their international status with characteristic humor. One official claims to be able to imitate almost every brand of African politician. He specializes in Dr. Nkrumah's colleagues: "I come from Ghana which used to be called the Gold Coast because people came to our coast and took away the gold. And I come here to Addis Ababa which means "new flower" but I have seen nothing new and no flowers."

The Ethiopians look on white visitors with the same quizzical humor. "They're amazing, these Americans," said a tourist official, "they go to so many different countries they can't remember where they are. I asked one man the other day which hotel he was staying in. He searched through a long notebook but couldn't find it. I think he'd forgotten the name of the city. You know, it's amazing how many Americans arrive in Ethiopia and ask to be shown the pyramids." But because of their self-confidence, the Ethiopians are free from the nasty and boring color neurosis that poisons so much of the continent. In most African states the country people will greet the Europeans with blank or hostile stares. In Ethiopia they will laugh, smile, shake hands, and try to make him feel welcome. This can happen in parts of West Africa but is rare. Travel bores rank Ethiopia with

KENYA: Ray Ryan, joint owner (with actor William Holden) of the Mount Kenya Safari Club

SOUTHERN RHODESIA: Pupils at the Mount Pleasant Boys' School

TANZANIA: Israeli construction engineers in front of a hotel

SOUTHERN RHODESIA: In Salisbury, Tim Wood runs his own private army of security guards.

ANGOLA: José Cagido, on his coffee plantation near the Congolese border

CONGO: Belgian miner in Katanga

MOZAMBIQUE: Alfredo Pereira and his family near Nampula

SOUTH AFRICA: An Afrikaner (Boer) farmer of the Orange Free State

Thailand for the amiabilty of its people. And Thailand, also a clerical monarchy, is the only country in its part of the world that has never known colonization. The sense of racial equality is good for the Ethiopians. It also makes life far more pleasant for white people who do not here find themselves obliged to take up poses of arrogance or false chumminess.

Again in contrast to most of Africa, there is widespread mixing sexually between the whites and blacks. Coleridge is not the only man to have sung the beauties of the "Abyssinian maid." The Arabs and Turks prized them highly as girl slaves not only because of their beautiful faces and bodies but because, so it was said, their skin was cool to the touch, even in scorching weather. Their women are still as lovely as ever, and far more free. There is none of the subjugation or timidity so often found in eastern countries. Indeed, the Ethiopians are notably forward in matters of sex. "I gave terrible offense to one guy here," said a G.I., "because I didn't realize he understood English. I'd just asked a friend of mine if all the women in Ethiopia were whores. It was a fair question. We'd been driving for two days and this buddy of mine—he's really girl crazy—would just stop the car every time he saw an attractive girl and they'd go off into the bushes. Not one of them refused him." This may have been simply a G.I.'s fantasy, but it corresponds to most travelers' impressions of Ethiopia. And Europeans fall readily into the same behavior pattern and, as in Kenya, blame the altitude. Ethiopian men have almost as much success with European women. Even the high V.D. rate does not deter lechery. "I don't believe those stories," said an enthusiastic Welshman in Addis Ababa. "They always put them around when there's a particularly lovely variety of local woman."

All in all, Ethiopia is a welcoming land to foreigners—and they have come in their tens of thousands. The Indians help train the army; the British and Norwegians the navy; the Americans and Swedes the air force. The Austrians run hotels, the French manage the railway, the Yugoslavs provided a port and the Bulgarians a fishing fleet. The Czechs make shoes, the Italians beer and the Japanese shirts. The Russians have built an oil refinery and the People's Republic of China gave an Economic Reconstruction Exhibition in a corrugated iron shack now littered with garbage.

By diversifying his foreign advisers, the Emperor has acquired some of the benefits of colonialism without losing his independence. He carries this policy of "divide and be ruled" to great lengths of subtlety. He tries to prevent politically friendly powers—such as the British and Americans—from co-operating on any particular aid project. He would prefer to see, say, the Yugoslavs and West Germans joined in an uneasy alliance. He thus prevents his many advisers from ganging up on him. It also keeps the different foreigners fighting hard for Ethiopian favor. It is easy to tell the advisers and experts who really take their jobs seriously. They suffer from tapeworms. This is the penalty for joining the Ethiopians in their own traditional feasts of raw meat. "A splendid man," said one ambassador of his information officer, "he went all round the country and got more tapeworms than he could count."

The influence of Britain has decreased over the years. Things started to go wrong in 1941 when the British Army advisers on politics tended to treat Ethiopia more as a protectorate than as a liberated ally. After the war many British people left in a huff. Once all the secondary school headmasters had been British. Now there are few British teachers at all. The British Council withdrew its office in 1951 during a Whitehall wave of economy. When they asked the Emperor to the reopening in 1958, he replied rather sharply that he had already opened the offices once but would be glad to pay a visit when they were functioning properly. The Council still need the go-ahead to open a branch office in Asmara, the second city.

"Omo is available throughout the Empire of Ethiopia," say the placards for this British soap detergent. The same could not be said of British influence. True, the Ethiopian army still wear solar topees that date to the British raj—and they give their words of command in very British English. The Addis Ababa fops get their cavalry twill trousers, their suede boots and their cocktail party gossip from the King's Road, Chelsea, London. An English mission up-country still busies itself with one of the most imbecilic tasks in the world: the conversion of Ethiopian Jews to the Ethiopian Orthodox Church. But British exports to Ethiopia lag behind Italy, West Germany and the United States. The Peace Corps, with more than five hundred teachers in Ethiopia, has taken over the English teaching in schools. "Why don't the Americans want to teach with English books?" I was asked by a schoolboy in Dire Dawa. "In Ethiopia we always preferred English books and pronunciation. But most of our teachers are Peace Corps. The others are Indians and with them, if we say 'yeah' instead of 'yes' they tell us 'your're learning English, not American.' Why doesn't England herself send us some teachers?" The Assistant Minister of Education gave the answer: "Britain doesn't subsidize them and they're too expensive." Even the Church complains of British coldness. A delegate to a conference last year complained afterwards: "I felt sorry that the Anglican Church did not take more interest in the Ethiopian Orthodox Church. It is the one Western Church that could recognize us as the Catholic Church in Ethiopia. That is not the attitude of the Roman Catholic Church or the other Protestant bodies."

Declining British influence in Ethiopia may be partly explained by Britain's need to concentrate aid to members of the Commonwealth. Probably it suits Haile Selassie's interests to accept more aid from countries that have never been tarred with the brush of colonialism: the Israelis, the West Germans, the Yugoslavs and the Russians. Sometimes these different nations find themselves almost in competition. At Harar, for instance, a town of forty thousand, there are four hospitals run by four different powers, including the Czechs and the Yugoslavs. There are even two rival leper colonies—one of mud huts run by a Frenchman and one of fine cement houses run by West Germans.

The strangest of all rivalries between the white people of Africa is to be found in the tiny township of Bahardar, on Lake Tana, where the Blue Nile begins its 2,750-mile journey down to the sea. This immense lake, six thousand feet above sea level, has a sacred and rather ominous role in Ethiopian history and mythology. There are still medieval monasteries on some of the islands, monasteries so strict that not even female animals are allowed to land. The town of Bahardar is intended to be the economic center of Ethiopia. There are few signs of it yet. The straggling settlements of mud huts support only fifteen thousand people, most of them peasants, and one textile mill run by Indians. The broad main street, made of the earth and dust of Africa, is little more than a forest clearing. Goats trot among the big sycamores, the banana and the bottle trees. A few priests squat by the conical, thatched church, trying halfheartedly to cadge a few cents from the passers-by. The midday heat is intense and the sun gives a harsh glow to the crude, dark colors of green, brown and red. Hornbills, herons, and pepper-and-salt colored wagtails fish in the puddles and marshland beside the lake, which is riddled with bilharzia. This fact does not worry the locals who fetch the water in tall pots to use in the washing and cooking. There is a grass strip for the visiting airplanes, but few passengers board or land at Bahardar. There were four of us on my last trip: John Bulmer, an airline worker, and one very airsick sheep. Bahardar is a most improbable battlefield of the cold war. Yet here four nations have striven in often ludicrous rivalry to impress their beliefs and attitudes on the indifferent locals.

Like almost every town in Ethiopia, Bahardar has its representatives of the Peace Corps, in this case William and Mary Chartrand, from Wisconsin and Michigan, respectively. They had married just after leaving college in 1964 and, two weeks later, enrolled for Peace Corps training at U.C.L.A. "They warned us that we'd feel very depressed after three months," said Chartrand, "and I guess we expected it." When I met them, almost exactly three months after coming to Bahardar, they were not depressed so much as "very, very exhausted. We start school at a quarter to nine and go on till five-thirty. And there's so much to do at home. When we got off that plane at Addis we were on our own. We stayed at the Ras Hotel for more than a month before we moved into a house. It's got a pump in the garden but now the water's turned off and we have to get it all from the lake and then boil it. Then there's the cooking. Everything needs cooking."

Nor was teaching school without difficulties. "Sometimes it's really difficult not to start criticizing," Chartrand said. "For instance, you come in and find that half the class is kneeling outside the door for the whole period just because they were one minute late. And the punishment's very severe. They use the stick and the leather whip. But we don't have many problems over discipline. It's all right in the provinces. But in Addis, if they don't like what you're doing the kids just go on strike. They walk out on you. But here we just can't get used to the way they all stand up when you walk into the classroom. We don't do that back in the States."

There are three other Americans in Bahardar—U.S. Air Force personnel taking part in a mapping mission of Ethiopia. They send up balloons to record winds, temperature and humidity but have most of their six-month stay to spend on the social life of Bahardar. The sergeant, a colored man, and one of the two white airmen are bachelors and patronize the three ramshackle clubs. The third man, John Baker, is married and prefers to pass his evenings sipping tea at the hotel. There is no shortage of conversation. As the only Texan and Goldwater supporter in Bahardar, Baker takes part in a kind of serialized argument with the four or five Ethiopian regulars at the Ras Hotel bar.

The West, or the Free World, or what you will, is further represented at Bahardar by three doctors, two nurses and one technician from West Germany who run the hospital on the west side of town. This staff, with seventy beds, has to serve five hundred thousand people. "They bring them in on their beds from twenty or thirty miles away," said Dr. Friedrich Schaeuffele, the superintendent. "My colleagues were afraid that they would not have enough work to do here but there are waiting lists three months long for operations." The hospital is a gift of the German Federal government to the Ethiopian Ministry of Public Health. The German staff signed on for three years, two years ago. After that, said Dr. Schaeuffele, it will revert to Ethiopian hands, "but in this country there are only twenty-nine doctors." He is a big, bluff Bavarian who has worked seven years in the country, after a previous seven years in Iran. "A doctor here should be married," he said. "To send a young doctor here alone is a heavy imposition. And a doctor should be ready for compromise. Not to be too exact. Not to believe there's an easy solution."

The patients at Dr. Schaeuffele's hospital suffer from "all the diseases you have in Europe and some special diseases. One special problem is the malnutrition of infants," and he showed me a room full of sick children, each tied by its skinny hands to the sides of the cot. "Do you see that? Malnutrition, not hunger. Malnutrition. The mothers keep them breast feeding until they are three and then when their milk runs out they don't know what to feed them. Do you see this little one here? All yellow. And at one year he's the same weight as at birth . . . We don't let the mothers in with them. If we did, the whole town would be in here. We're not like Albert Schweitzer at Lambarene. We have to be strict, and we only have seventy beds. We can't take any more. Not enough doctors. Not enough money."

Not far from Bahardar the Blue Nile roars over the Tisisat Falls, which Alan Moorehead has called "the grandest spectactle that either the Blue or the White Nile has to offer." Since he wrote that phrase in his incomparable *The Blue Nile*, a Yugoslav engineering company has built a barrage on the west side of the river just above the falls which can divert part or all the flow of the stream into a hydroelectric turbine. The loss to natural beauty, in Ethiopian eyes, is more than compensated by a supply of electricity for the industry that may one day reach Bahardar.

The barrage was not aid in the strictest sense of the word. The Yugoslavs have a special relationship with the Ethiopians which has little to do with ideology. It happens that Tito and Haile Selassie are two energetic old men with a shared hobby: gadding about the world on state visits. The Marxist-Leninist marshal was the first head of state ever to visit Ethiopia, and Yugoslavia was, in turn, the first Communist state to be visited by the Conquering Lion of the Tribe of Judah, Elect of God and King of the Kings of Ethiopia. The Elect of God and the Elect of the League of Communists get on famously. The Ethiopians are pleased to do business with Yugoslavia, a seemingly neutralist country. The Yugoslavs, who are surrounded by tariff walls in Europe, look for profits from Ethiopia. Since business in Yugoslavia is highly competitive, at least three engineering companies offered tenders to get the Tisisat Falls contract. The Workers' Council controlling the company then took the decision to accept the contract. Wages and salaries in the company would depend on whether or not this project, thousands of miles away, would be finished within the allotted time. But Workers' Councils have no control over the actual work in progress. "The orders here are given by the chief engineer," said Misha Zubradovic, the chief engineer, "and when you're on a project like this, time is very important. But the Workers' Council made the decision to acept the contract." African life has not been too hard for Zubradovic. He has a comfortable bungalow, a trim garden of dazzling tropical flowers, a portrait of Marshal Tito on the bedroom wall, and several varieties of Scotch in the drink cabinet. Moreover, his wife and child enjoy it too. "It's better here for the women than for the men," he said, "they have time to read a bit and relax."

Although a score of Yugoslavs had been working on this project, most of the labor was Ethiopian. "It was, how shall I find the right word, unlearned," said Zubradovic. "It was so-so. They have little experience, except for the ones who have done practical work in Yugoslavia." Some of Zubradovic's colleagues were less restrained in their comments on Ethiopia when we met them one night at the Gondar Bar, one of the three mud-walled brothel-cum-drinking-dens which Bahardar affords. Girls with beautiful names like Lemlem, wearing medieval national dress, danced with the customers for a bottle of beer a time. A bearded tailor, in jodhpurs and flowing burnous, squatted low in the twist while wagging his right forefinger heavenward—for all the world like a tight Biblical prophet. The three Yugoslavs were celebrating their departure. One of them, always hostile to other foreigners, had now turned malevolent. "Get out of here," he muttered, then ostentatiously took a revolver out of his pocket. His two colleagues had taken up positions behind the bar, and were pouring out their troubles: "You think the Ethiopians are good people? They're 100 per cent bad. A man goes to study for one year and he thinks he can be an engineer . . . They're worse than the Montenegrins. The Montenegrins are more advanced but in some ways they're even worse than the Ethiopians. But that's politics." The surly man with the gun then came over to break up the conversation. All three were Croatians with that air of superiority which the advanced Catholic Yugoslavs often show to their poorer, Orthodox fellow countrymen.

During a visit to Russia in 1960, the Emperor Haile Selassie asked how the country had managed to make such advances in less than fifty years. "Technical education," said the Russians, and offered to build him a technical college in Ethiopia. The result, in its second year of operation, stands near to the source of the Blue Nile at Bahardar. The half dozen buildings in gleaming glass and colored panels blend awkwardly with the red dust road, the thatched mud huts and the villagers in medieval robes. But there is no denying the excellence of the equipment: tractors, lathes, grinders, electrical measurement machines, a well-stocked chemistry laboratory. The government planned to take two hundred and fifty boys a year up to a maximum of a thousand after four years, but after two years there were still only four hundred pupils.

The eighteen Russians, including four women interpreters, are there as advisers to twenty-seven Ethiopian teachers who actually do the teaching. In theory they merely explain the Russian equipment but in practice they often have to help out with the actual teaching. Some of the Ethiopian teachers are barely qualified. A lecturer in chemistry is a physics undergraduate at Addis

Ababa who is teaching from what he remembered of school chemistry. Undoubtedly, all the Russians knew their technical jobs and how to handle the equipment.

Almost inevitably there have been troubles. At first the Russians had wanted the teaching done in Amharic and the "advice" given in Russian. This soon proved unworkable, and English is now the language almost throughout. "Students will not steal time between classes," says one of the all-English announcements pinned on the notice board; even the Russian films shown in the main hall have to be given English subtitles. None of the Russians I met spoke Amharic; few had more than a smattering of English. On the other hand, nine of the Ethiopian lecturers had started to learn Russian and one, with characteristic African flair for languages, spoke it quite well. "The pronunciation is just like Amharic," he said.

If the Russians had ever hoped to use their technical college for straight political aims, the intent was frustrated. The lack of communication made this almost inevitable. True, the very magnificence of the college and its equipment may have given some Ethiopians a rosy idea of the U.S.S.R. The Russian scientific textbooks, in English editions, back up the Party line. "The U.S.S.R. was again the first country. . . ." said one boastful work on physics, while a history of chemistry was illustrated with portraits only of (Tsarist) Russian inventors. But there are even more Western than Russian textbooks. The Assistant Director of the College, Ato Million Belete, was anxious to get even more from British publishers. His own ideological neutrality stood revealed in the two calendars hanging above his desk. One, from Russia, showed a Sovcolor view of the Moscow Canal. The other, from an Addis Ababa bookseller, showed a waxen-faced Christ gazing lugubriously at a robin. The Ethiopians have the first and last word on any decisions affecting politics. For instance, they invited the U.S.I.S. man, Phelon Peters, whom I had met in Uganda, to lecture at the college on America's space program. "The students there didn't seem to have been exposed to Russian influence," said Peters.

Most of the Russians I met in Bahardar seemed very decent, friendly people. They got on well with the students and approved of their industry, but their relationship seemed formal. There was little joking—once again because of the language problem. "We play football with the students, of course," said one of the younger Russians, Anatoly Novoselov, from Tashkent, "but not much because of the altitude." None of the Russians here had previously left the U.S.S.R. and some of them seem to suffer badly from homesickness. "It's fun for a few weeks—but for a year, Ech!" was one comment. Only a few of them have been able to bring their families, although all are allowed at least one long leave during their three-year stint. Their letters from Russia take three weeks, but *Pravda* arrives in four days. Cold comfort.

The Russians are childishly pleased that the word for tea, "chaj," is the same in Amharic and Russian. They frequently order it just for the pleasure of being understood. It pleases them still more that one of the tiny "duccas" or shops in the town is called Gum, like the immense state department store opposite the Kremlin. They all patronize Bahardar's Gum and especially its checked, Afrika-Corps-style, peaked caps—imported from Japan. "It's our uniform," one of them told us. "They all know we're Russians because of it." Some of them have become old Africa hands. They take a boat out on the lake to angle for catfish or visit the monasteries. They hike on the mountains. The three who kindly drove us out to the Tisisat Falls one morning were expert guides to the wildlife—"Here you will see apes"—and to the local history—"This is the place where His Imperial Majesty had his lunch." The scruffy guard who tried to demand baksheesh from Alexander Shumikov got choked off with the kind of rebuke that might have come from the lips of any old settler. But in one respect they refuse to go African: "I have tried this meat which is not roasted," said the woodwork adviser, "but it is dangerous."

The four white nations in remote Bahardar keep rather aloof from each other. The Yugoslavs who are left after the barrier was completed still get on well with the Russians. For instance, Mrs. Zubradovic speaks fluent Russian and Mr. Zubradovic greets the Russian Shumikov with a smacking kiss—Slav style. The two groups combine for fishing or hiking expeditions. Some of the Yugoslavs struck up a friendship with the German nurses at the hospital and would appear for a drink in the bar of the Ras Hotel. But otherwise there is little social contact.

"The Germans here are very nice," said William Chartrand of the Peace Corps. "The Russians we haven't really met to talk to. They've been having trouble with the Germans. They invited them to a film show and it was a war film, very anti-German, so the Germans walked out." The German Dr. Schaeuffele told the story differently. "The Russians used to come up here very often. Not socially, but to bring their families to the hospital. Then, after Khrushchev's dismissal, they stopped coming. They took the hard line. I'm sure this was political. They are very nice people, though. But rather suspicious."

One of the U.S. airmen, John Baker, had discovered the same thing: "I went over to see two of the Russian secretaries the first week I was here. I wanted to buy some vodka from them because vodka is the only thing I like to drink. They gave me some tea and we had a talk and I asked them to call on us. But they never called in to see us and never asked us back again." Just as he said this two of the Russians entered the bar. I had asked them over for a beer and they seemed pleased at getting an evening out from their big Russian hostel. Then Baker, who had acquired some U.S. vodka to celebrate his wedding anniversary, invited us to drink with him. The party went well. "Made in U.S.A.," shouted one of the Ethiopians, after examining the bottle. "They have stolen your vodka," he explained to the two Russians. He then launched into a general denunciation of both the U.S.A. and the U.S.S.R. for having turned away from Christianity. The Russians took the traditional way out of any embarrassing scene. "Let us drink to peace," they said, which we did. Then a party of Swedish missionaries, who had arrived that day by coach, started to sing "Holy Night" and other carols outside, to the intense irritation of everybody—Russian, American, Ethiopian and British. The party grew argumentative once again and this time the Russians delivered their other toast: "To the exploration of space."

Outside in the fresh air, it all seemed suddenly ludicrous. A dove chanted its warning "whoop-whoop-whoop"; some small animal screamed in the night; the fireflies danced like specks in the eye, and the waves lapped on the shore of strange Lake Tana. To hell with exploring space, I thought, when there's still Africa.

Rhodesia

IN MOMENTS of anguish Cecil Rhodes, the empire builder, would ask his friend Rudyard Kipling, "What am I trying to say, Ruddy? What am I trying to say?" The remark might well serve as a motto for the anguished white community of present Southern Rhodesia. They have got themselves in a fine mess, and they cannot think how to escape from it. The Central African Federation failed because most of the whites wished to interpret it in Lord Malvern's revealing phrase as "the relationship between a rider and a horse." The 221,000 whites can never feel comfortable trying to hold down four million increasingly restive Africans. They can expect nothing more than moral support from South Africa, which does not want to add Rhodesia's black population to her own. Torn between the desire for independence from British nagging and a fear of losing British economic help, the Southern Rhodesians wobble between the extremist Smith and the more moderate Welensky. Whatever their doubts, they are certain of one thing: life is good for the whites in Southern Rhodesia. They want to keep it that way for as long as possible.

The history of the whites in Southern Rhodesia is comparable to the first three parts of Wagner's *Ring of the Niebelungen.* They came in search of gold, overthrew the existing race by cunning and treachery, and now behave as though crazed by the Niebelung curse. The parallel could be pursued, but falls down in two respects: we have still to wait for the twilight of these gods, and Mr. Ian Smith makes a shabby Siegfried. Only Rhodes himself was a figure of true Wotan stature. Whatever the ethics of his conquest of Central Africa, he always thought and acted big.

Rhodesia began with a swindle. In 1888, Lobengula, last king of the Matabele warriors, was tricked by Rhodes's agents into signing away the metal and mineral rights of Matabeleland for £100 a month, a thousand rifles, ammunition and a gunboat—which last he did not receive. The concession went only to Rhodes's company. When Lobengula learned from the missionaries the nature of the contract he had signed he sent emissaries to London to revoke the document and to appeal to the white Queen. Much of British public opinion was also suspicious of Rhodes's slick maneuvers. But Rhodes himself outsmarted the simple Africans. By playing on British imperial longings, by lying promises of concern for the natives, and sometimes by plain bribery, he managed to win support for his drive north from South Africa. Once Rhodes had won his royal charter for the British South Africa Company to develop the new territories, he organized, in 1890, the Pioneer Column for the march north. These two hundred English and Afrikaner whites, backed by three hundred coloreds and Africans, hoisted the Union Jack at what is now Salisbury on September 13, 1890. Within three years fighting had broken out between the Rhodesians and the depleted kingdom of Lobengula. One foray has grown into the folk legend of modern Southern Rhodesia. It is the story of how a mounted patrol, under Major Allan Wilson, crossed the Shangani River to reconnoiter the African camp. Instead of returning, as ordered, these thirty-three men of the Shangani Patrol launched an attack on Lobengula's three thousand warriors—and were very naturally killed. The reckless and unnecessary death of the Shangani Patrol is the Siegfried motif in the "Ring of the Rhodesians." The final triumph of the whites came in 1896 with the crushing of another revolt by the Mashonas and Matabele.

The British Government failed from the very start to exercise control over the new Rhodesians. They allowed the British South Africa Company to administer the territory from 1889 until 1922, when the settlers themselves voted to become a self-governing colony. This was the beginning of disaster, because it meant that the British Government could not easily intervene to impose its will on the settlers. Above all, it could not oblige them to share power and prosperity with their African subjects. This was why the Central African Federation was doomed from the start to collapse. The Africans in Northern Rhodesia and Nyasaland wanted a part in government and were able to win this from Whitehall.

The white Southern Rhodesians could manage their own State as they wished, but could not impose their racism on the other two territories. Hence the emergence of Southern Rhodesia as a semi-independent white state, with a Government edging always rightwards via Whitehead and Field to Smith. They tell the world that uncertainty about Southern Rhodesia's future has checked immigration, stultified business and caused much suffering to the small man. But life is still good—for the whites.

A white man in Salisbury gets about one and a half times as much for the job as his equivalent in England. Moreover, by virtue of color and because of the shortage of trained Africans, he can generally get a better job than he would in England, where he would face greater competition. It would probably be fair to say that the Salisbury white gets paid about twice as much as he is worth. The white Southern Rhodesians constantly tell you that Africans to the north have proved incapable of administering their independent countries. In fact, one is struck in Salisbury by the startling incompetence of the Europeans. The rude, lazy hotel staff, the shopgirls who cannot add, the airline staff who misread your ticket are all imcompetent even by African standards. But they retain their jobs because customers prefer to be served by whites and because there are few Africans qualified to replace them. The whites make sure of that. It is symptomatic of Smith's Administration that he has actually raised fees for African schools.

The manager of a firm that supplies secretarial staff

informed me: "The average salary for a shorthand typist is £60–£65 a month. The seniors get anything from £65–£75, and the really topnotch secretary gets anything from £85–£100 . . . About 90 per cent of all married women go out to work, mostly because they have to. They're in bond over houses, they want to send their children to private schools, or they spend an awful lot on clothes, although the cost of living isn't high . . . It's a question of keeping up standards. But then there are quite a lot who go out to work even although they don't need to. The servants look after the children; they can't play tennis all day; they get bored . . ." According to employers in Salisbury, these same secretaries expect to finish work by lunchtime and are very reluctant to earn their high fees. In addition to high wages and salaries, most white Southern Rhodesians pay little tax.

With incomes as good as this, it is not surprising to find an article in *At Home in Rhodesia* claiming that "the building of a private pool is now within the reach of most property owners." Indeed, Kenneth Humphries, managing director of the Outdoor Living Center, said proudly, 'They did a survey nine months ago and found that, next to Beverly Hills, we had the highest number of swimming pools per head—Europeans, of course—of anywhere in the world . . . We follow American trends, and you'll find that our pools follow exactly the American pattern." A look through the brochure showed that among the more modest pools were the Rectangle, Mirror, Crescent, Gem, Angelo and Laguna, while the *de luxe* pool shapes include the Siesta, Woodlands, Canada, Monaco and Roman. There are four thousand pools in Salisbury—proportionately more than the eighteen thousand in northern Johannesburg—or one pool for every five families. "We build for lots of salaried people," said Mr. Humphries, "such as flight engineers on Central African Airways, minor bank officials and storekeepers. Then, of course, more than half of all farmers have pools. People regard it as just as normal as having a car. Literally, every garden in the Highlands suburb has a pool, and it's just like having a garage . . . In the last three years we have seen a progressive increase in the number of people starting pools. In spite of all that's happened, people are still prepared to spend five hundred to eight hundred pounds to help them to enjoy what they've got . . . Last year our program was eight pools a month. This year it will be ten pools a month."

Pools are built in the winter and take from Monday morning till Saturday to install. The swimming season starts in the third week of August and lasts until the end of April. The running costs are about £3 a month for chemicals and 7s 6d. for electricity. Once the first investment has been made—and the cheapest pool costs £400—it is therefore quite cheap to maintain. Also, of course, it raises the price of the house, and Mr. Humphries's firm has put in a number of pools for landlords just to help them let their houses. "It's patio living," Mr. Humphries explained to me. "It goes with barbecues, outdoor furniture in plastic and metal, easy tables, and perhaps a gay umbrella. We show people how to live."

Over and over again one hears white Rhodesian

women say, "My houseboys are so hopeless that I might just as well do the job myself to start with." They never do. Some households get by with the "rock-bottom" number of two servants. The average is about four, paid an average £4 a month each. Since the housewives do not really have to spend as much time as they make out in supervising the servants, there is plenty of spare energy for tennis, parties and bridge. "The women here are the laziest in the world," said a non-Rhodesian housewife. Also, perhaps, rather bored. An article on the woman's page of the *Rhodesia Herald* asked, "Are we all sleepyheads? . . . Ask your friends and you will find a large number are in bed by 8:30 or 9 P.M. . . . Three young girls whose ages range from twenty to twenty four each told me that they are always in bed by 8:30 except Friday and Saturday nights, when they go to the cinema or dancing. 'Nothing else to do,' said one. 'I'm too sleepy,' said the other two." The article reported that a Salisbury doctor, who himself went to bed between 9 and 10:00 could offer no medical reason for this. My own inquiries bore out the evidence about early bedtimes. The explanation is surely boredom.

Although 90 per cent of white Southern Rhodesians live in the towns, they still like to imagine themselves as intrepid settlers—heirs of the men who came with the covered wagons and fought in the Shangani Patrol. The nearest thing to them today is the tobacco farmer. Compared with most kinds of agriculture, this is quite easy work which can be left for months on end to a moderately capable manager. The intrepid, pioneering qualities become necessary for borrowing money to finance the next season's crop. In spite of warnings of overproduction in 1963, many new people borrowed the money to farm tobacco, with the result that prices were down last September to 22d. a pound, which is hardly enough to cover expenses. Many people were expected to go bankrupt. But then, bankruptcy has no stigma in Southern Rhodesia, and many people have lost three or four fortunes on tobacco. "I was married to a tobacco planter for six years," said Penny McCallum-Brown, who does public relations work for one of the three Salisbury tobacco auction rooms, "and I wouldn't do it again for anything. It's a laugh if you've got a sense of humor, and I have. But I think I'm better off working here now." Tobacco farmers generally come in to watch the bidding and I saw few signs of the necessary humor. As the buyers shuffle along in a crocodile to feel and sniff at the leaf on sale, the auctioneer rattles off a gibberish commentary on the bids, moving the price downward in pennies or upward in half-pennies per pound weight. If the buyer is dissatisfied with the tobacco, he tears up the ticket of purchase—a disgrace to the farmer concerned. One farmer with two torn tickets marked to his name this year was so ashamed that he sent his wife in to supervise the sale—a tough-looking woman in tweeds whom only the bravest buyer would want to offend.

About one third of the farmers come from South Africa. One of these, Mike Riquebourg, told me that last year he had put his entire savings in a tobacco farm and was naturally cast down at hitting a bad year straight off. "Getting an overdraft from a bank is a terrible job. Honestly, we only exist by playing off one bank against another. The capital you have to invest is fantastic—about £120 an acre at least." Interest to the banks or to a merchant comes at a minimum 8 per cent; and on top of this comes the worry of politics. I think there is a great future for the tobacco industry—even under an African Government. After all, the growers in Northern Rhodesia aren't worried by independence coming. But I think this Government [in Southern Rhodesia] should tell people one way or other what they want to do and what would happen to the tobacco industry if it went independent . . . The English have been good to us economically. The imperial preference comes to one and sixpence in the pound, and they've bought up a lot of our crop this year. Would they do that if we were independent?" Many Southern Rhodesians, who incline to Smith's views on the racial issue, are worried about the economic results of independence.

It may have been partly to keep this economic help that the Southern Rhodesians have broadcast the myth that the country was brought into poverty by the collapse of Federation. I had heard stories of half finished buildings left to rot in Salisbury; of weeds bursting up through the concrete, and of broken families trekking in desperation to South Africa. Certainly the country is not booming as hard as in the fifties, but there is no real sign of a slump. Take property, for example. "The peak as regards residential property was long before Federation," said Roy Barrier of Guest and Tanner, estate agents. "It was in the early fifties. Then it leveled out until about 1957. The shortage had been overcome, and there was a fairly big drop in copper revenue that year, which put the wind up people. Then we had a revival until the 'wind of change' speech—and that's precisely what it was. Then there was a transitional period until about eighteen months ago when people began to feel, 'Why shouldn't I buy?' Now there is quite an active market in houses, although prices are about 25 to 30 per cent below the peak." Nor is the story true that more than half the office space is empty. Mr. Barrier reckons the surplus space at about 10 per cent, and he pointed out that much of the phenomenal investment in building was "funk money" from the United Kingdom sent to Salisbury to avoid death duties. "Things are really looking up this year," he went on. "The Pearl Assurance Building was empty two years ago, and it's full now, although, mind you, the price is too low. Good office space is going at 1s.-1s. 3d. a square foot when it should be 2s." Housing is quite cheap by the standard of the continent. "One can rent a good detached house for £35 a month, or about 20 per cent of an average family income, while if they want to go to another area they can get it for £20 a month."

The Mayor of Salisbury, who this year chanced to be a pleasant and liberal man, Frank Clements, was cautiously optimistic about the city's future. "Greater Salisbury has approximately 300,000 people, of whom about 90,000 are Europeans. I wouldn't have put the loss of Europeans at more than four thousand since the breakdown of Federation. I would have said that the drop had stopped, that most of the people who were going have gone. But I don't think the gaps made by the exodus have yet been filled. You've got to remember that before 1959 we were developing faster than any city in the world." Things had picked up again, though. Rate income was higher, as was expenditure on building. "Salisbury is basically an agricultural town," the Mayor explained, "and our basic outlook is good because our agriculture is expanding. None of our industry depends, like Bulawayo's, on trade with the north."

The Mayor is very proud of the orderliness of Salisbury: "Really it's just like Surbiton, Surbiton set in Africa. The average Salisbury man is not a Wild Westerner. There have been no race riots here, even in the sense that you have them in London. We haven't got any 'Mods and Rockers.' Our 'First Street Cowboys' occasionally fight each other, but they don't fight the Africans. The trouble we've had in the African townships was from the Africans fighting each other, poor people." The removal of color bars in public places had not provoked any trouble from the whites, "but among the majority of white citizens there would be an objection to Africans living in the neighborhood." The Mayor made it clear that he did not himself agree with this attitude.

The Mayor of Salisbury and other fellow citizens went out of their way to say that theirs was not a "ghost town." Sometimes it seemed to me more like a town haunted by its present inhabitants. The Rhodesians, as the whites call themselves—they are the only whites in Africa to have taken even the national name from the natives—are a weirdly neurotic lot beneath their suntans. In the first place, they are obsessed by the myth of the pioneer, although most of them came to the country since the last war. The schoolboys wear wideawake hats in the style thought suitable to the veldt at the turn of the century. The grownups do annual homage to Rhodes and to the cairn of the fallen pioneers each "Occupation Day" or "Pioneer Day," as it is now called. Nobody laughed in a Salisbury public house one evening when a quite sober man stood to attention and sang "Goodbye," the self-pitying ballad of a legionary bound for Africa: "It's an Abyssinian French Division . . . I shall do my bit," and so on through sentiments so treacly as to be ludicrous. It is an interesting contrast to Kenya, where most of the white settlers really have experienced the ardors and dangers of pioneering, but generally try to play down the legend. The Southern Rhodesian whites are often aggressive to English people, but without any confidence in their cause. "What are we going to do?" they keep asking, rather as Rhodes asked Kipling what he was trying to say.

Fear aggravates the bewilderment. Although there has been no concerted black terrorism against the whites, there has been plenty of unpleasantness. Africans frequently hurl stones at passing cars. There are more cases of mugging than could be explained by purely criminal motives. There is quite considerable burglary in Salisbury. With the suppression of all legal political action by

Africans there is a danger of more violence to come, and the whites know this. This explains why the Police are white-officered, why the Army is almost entirely white and the Air Force completely white. It explains the creation of paramilitary groups of security guards. One of these, Salisbury Security Services, employs a hundred and twenty uniformed African guards and five Europeans who patrol business premises at night and do special guards for householders on holiday or with special fears of housebreaking. The head of the force, Tim Wood, is a tall red-bearded Welshman, ex-Grenadier Guards, ex-Shanghai, ex-Kenya Police, ex-Somaliland, who came down to Salisbury seven years ago. "They said I was too old to work, so I started this business just with three men and a bicycle. Now I have a hundred and twenty-five and bulldogs. The bulldogs collect for charity, you know. We had one collecting when Sir Roy Welensky came along, and he stopped and asked the name of the dog. We said it was Winston Welensky Junior, and Roy laughed so much he put a fiver in the box." Every evening Wood holds a parade of the African guards on duty, whom he drills with correct regimental barks. His line of business has good prospects of growth in Salisbury.

In principle, there has been removal of color restrictions in Salisbury. Discrimination may still persist in the really important matters of education, work and property. But some of the "pinpricks," as Sir Roy so discreetly called them, have been removed. Africans can now enter the best hotels, although they will not be made very welcome: even less welcome than the ordinary white guest, which is saying something. They can now be served at the counter of any shop rather than having to go round to a hatch at the side. Here again they are often treated with impudence by the English sales staff, who clearly regret the days when the customer was always white. Mixing is now legal, but this only serves to exaggerate the hostility. For instance, the blacks are by law allowed into any bar. In practice they have been given their own bars. One adjoins the bar where I spent several evenings in Salisbury. "It's like if I was in London," said one of the regular customers, "I wouldn't go for a drink in the Savoy. I wouldn't stay in Mayfair, right? And they don't want to mix with us. They have a bar next door. It's a bigger bar than this one. If one of them was to come in here he wouldn't be welcome. He wouldn't be served. He'd be shown his own bar. It's like you have the four-ale bar in the U.K. Nobody wants to change that, do they?" Unfortunately for the susceptibilities of the customers, they are obliged to share the lavatories with the blacks. "It's first on the right and along the corridor," yelled a regular to his drinking companion, "but open the door carefully in case there's a kaffir in it."

The Speke Bar itself has a Scottish air about it, with hand and foot railings to lean on, Cornish pasties on sale, barmaids behind the counter but no women allowed the other side. "There's been nothing but depressing news here for five years," said Rosie, one of the barmaids. "If I was to win first prize in the lottery I wouldn't spend it here I can tell you straight." Another evening the other barmaid handed to one of the customers a clipping about Southern Rhodesia from the London *Sunday Express.* It was headed "Englishmen? I'd punch their faces." The barmaid gave a tch-tch as she thought about it. "It says we want to shoot all the Africans." The customer read the article very slowly and handed it back with a sigh. "I see they've got a typhoid epidemic there in the U.K.," he remarked. The barmaid said, "Yes. It's terrible in this day and age." A maudlin gentleman next to me said he was desperately worried by shortage of engineering workers. He was so worried he went out drinking at nights. He had come up here from South Africa: "But I couldn't stick the Republic. After all, there might be a couple of blokes speak to you in a pub, and they'd be talking Afrikaans. You pick up the phone and the operator speaks to you in Afrikaans. I wouldn't want to go back."

In his admirable *Politics of Partnership*, Mr. Patrick Keatley writes that it "was not a cross-section of Victorian England that emigrated to Rhodesia; the intellectuals, the aristocrats and the social reformers stayed at home." Because so many white Southern Rhodesians have a poor educational background they find it more difficult than the white Kenyans to understand the changes in Africa. The manual workers tend to be more racialistic than their white-collar countrymen. In the same bar a copy boy on the *Rhodesia Herald* pointed contemptuously to a couple of journalists: "They're reporters, and it's f——ing crap they write. It's always one-sided, innit, the *Herald?* Always against the Government, aren't they?" I said that the *Herald* sounded to me very pale in its criticism of Smith, but the copy boy, a middle-aged, purple-faced man, was not listening: "After all, the rest of Africa is going Communist, innit? It's all going to the f——ing blacks? I mean they're not f——ing educated, are they? And then I get the local weekly papers sent over from home in Wales, and what do I find? This f——ing Labor M.P. is writing these things against Southern Rhodesia and South Africa."

Coon, kaffir, munt and nigger are the words commonly used by white Southern Rhodesians about their black fellow citizens. They seldom hesitate to use these words when black people are listening. They frequently tell funny racist stories. "Have you heard the latest one about Dr. Banda?" asked a tobacco salesman. "Apparently the day after the independence of Malawi he received a delegation of apes who had come to complain that the Africans were stealing their mealies." The social and economic status of the whites in Southern Rhodesia makes sense only if it is true that the white man is by nature superior to the black. The whites try to believe this and constantly look for reassurance from outside. "But you've got to admit they're inferior to us," they insist. If you do not reply, they repeat the question with almost neurotic intensity: "Don't you agree that the coons are inferior?" Only a prudent dislike of violence kept me from saying, "They couldn't be."

There is something guilty about their attitude to the blacks. Since one third of the population comes from

South Africa, many Southern Rhodesians suspect that the blacks are worse off here than in the Republic. My engineer acquaintance kept harking back to this: "They treat the coons better in the Republic than we do here. They look after them like babies. There were two coons in my factory in Jo'burg earning seventeen or eighteen quid a week. But if they step out of line they get clobbered. Mind you, 90 per cent of them are quite happy. It works out well."

The dislike and fear of the blacks is aggravated by ignorance. Only in the country is there any communication, and then of a rather paternalistic kind. "The Africans are intimidated by their political parties," said a South African-born tobacco farmer; "in fact, one of my boys is a member of both parties so he can show them either card, if they ask for it. But the Africans on the farms aren't so afraid. They're ignorant and they like to listen to rumors, but they're not intimidated. I like Africans. After all, I wouldn't be growing tobacco if it wasn't for Africans. We're all Rhodesians, after all, and we've got to work together. And the Africans on the farms are happy. They get enough money for their needs, and if they got any more they wouldn't save it. One of my boys spends all his money in two days. I asked him why and he said, 'Money is for white man, baas. We Africans just spend it.' " The same farmer warned me a few minutes later not to listen to what Africans told me because "they'll tell you anything they think you want to believe."

The whites and blacks in Salisbury scarcely mix at all.

The only whites to visit the black townships are policemen, officials, and social workers. The mass of the white population talk to no blacks except their servants. On my second day in the country I went to talk to a white political leader who began with the usual crack about "coming to tell us how to run our country." Throughout the interview he talked with tolerant, rather patronizing confidence. But at the end he suddenly lowered his voice and asked me, in the tones of a stranger in town wanting to find the nearest brothel, "Tell me, what are the Africans thinking?" I looked at him in amazement. "How should I know? I've only just arrived. This is your country." Yet the same question was put to me over and over again during my stay in Southern Rhodesia, always by people who lived there and often by people who claimed loudly to "understand the African."

The extraordinary truth dawned on me that these white Southern Rhodesians thought that I, a foreign journalist, was more likely than they, the inhabitants, to hear what 90 per cent of the nation were saying. This was later borne out by a few chance conversations with African clerks, servants or taxi drivers. They would begin by keeping silent or by making trivial conversation about the weather. As soon as I said I was not Rhodesian they became more talkative. One taxi driver tactfully asked to see my passport—"just out of curiosity"—before giving his views on Sir Roy Welensky. These views were unflattering. "The Rhodesians simply don't talk to us like you're talking to me," said the driver, "and we don't talk to them." Perhaps he was merely telling me what I wanted to hear.

There is, of course, what Sir Edgar Whitehead and other self-styled moderate whites call the "moderate African." There were a few of them at a meeting of the Rhodesian National Party when Sir Edgar gave one of his limp appeals to the nation. They stood nervously apart from the white supporters during the coffee and biscuits refreshments, and I cannot imagine what they can have thought of Sir Edgar's speech: "I can see nothing wrong in the maintenance of high standards . . . The steady loss of European population is becoming increasingly grave . . . The average European wage in real terms is less than it was in 1959." Most whites in Southern Rhodesia have acquired Sir Edgar's double talk. Standards means white supremacy. Moderate African means an African who agrees with Sir Edgar. African extremist means one who does not. About 90 per cent of the nation are extremist. The white community is so small and poor in talent that even people like Whitehead and Smith can become leaders, while a man of real skill like Welensky is promoted into an international figure. It is all the more surprising that they should waste this talent in bickering among themselves and forming splinter groups.

The European press and TV are cautious in debate. The *Rhodesia Herald* is mildly hostile to Smith in its editorial pages, but makes up for this with the continual whine of white extremism in its letter pages. The small RTV television station is equally unwilling to give offense. "We deliberately aim at a conservative news bulletin," said Robin Brown, who runs the "Tonight" program. "Quite frankly I wouldn't show rabid riot scenes. For instance, I won't show people being attacked by dogs. But anything else will go in, and we're protected by the fact that we've got a free press." When the S.R.B.C. tried to stop them giving too much publicity to a white liberal, the program demanded an official refusal, which, of course, made headlines in the papers next day. He sets great store by the integrity of the journalists. "The reporters who have come out here have brought with them the Western idea of a free press. But the present Government regards every journalist as a kind of weird intellectual or, as one man put it, 'as reeking, run-to-seed intellectuals.' " This was before the Smith Government suppressed the *Daily News*. The "Tonight" program has a staff of three, but goes out three nights a week. "We've got no trade unions here," Brown said, "and the news staff of RTV consists of thirteen people, including cameramen. I went to England at Christmas on a tour of TV stations, and they just wouldn't believe it . . . Also we make a fat profit. It's there to make profit."

One journalist told me, "I'm a liberal, but having moral principles is a very expensive luxury which few Europeans can afford." A sociologist opined that the average liberal-minded Englishman would lose these principles after five years of life in Southern Rhodesia. Another journalist, an Afrikaner, divided liberals up into three groups: the fake liberals, who pay lip service to multiracialism but in fact support white supremacy; the genuine liberals, among whom he included himself; and the sick liberals, like one Africa correspondent of a British newspaper, who started to hate all whites.

The dilemma of Southern Rhodesia is expressed most clearly, because most explicitly, at the University College in Salisbury. When Lord Salisbury himself came on a visit there last year some of the black students held up placards DO WE LOOK LIKE APES? and the right-wing whites held up placards YES. About one-third of the students are Africans, and most of the whites come from Rhodesia. It was started as a university for the whole Federation, and when Federation folded there was doubt about its future. The white extremists regarded it as a center of subversive liberalism—which in a way it is—and there was insufficient money to keep it. Since the Southern Rhodesians are averse to paying taxes, the British Government stepped in with a grant, and now even the white Rhodesians take some pride in their seat of higher learning. "The thing that moved me quite a lot," said the Principal, Walter Adams, "was going to a shop or to the barber's and hearing people say, 'They're not going to stop it, are they?' or, 'The University mustn't go.' "

The Principal told me a story which he thought spoke well for the University. "After a tea party recently there were three Africans and one white student left. The four got chatting, and the white boy, who is a second-year student, said, 'You know, I've changed my point of view a great deal in the last two years after thinking things over. I now realize the things I enjoy—a nice farm, a motorcar—and I'm going to fight for them. There's no moral basis for this. It's just that I like them.' Of course, the Africans were delighted by this. Of course, few people are as honest, particularly in front of Africans. But I think it's a very good thing that it should happen. It's only in this kind of atmosphere that you get that kind of exchange—from sharing classrooms, dining rooms, and games. This generation will be different men just because of the two or three years they have been here."

The Principal is evidently a liberal, but he frowns mildly on white students who carry liberalism to the extent of joining one of the African political parties: "They're rather an embarrassment. They don't really fit. The Africans don't really want them in their parties. They want to keep their parties clean, all black." The students I met in the dining room shared this view. "You can always tell the extreme liberal," said T.: "if there are Africans and Europeans sitting at opposite ends of the table, he'll come and sit with the Africans, whether they're his friends or not." That lunchtime the white and black students were, in fact, sitting in separate groups at table. The whites I spoke to were all liberals, but . . .

"I'd say almost a hundred per cent of the students here are liberals—when they arrive," said T. "I was utterly liberal three years ago, but I've been swinging slowly all the way. More of them will change if things get bad: a rock in the windscreen at sixty m.p.h. makes a man think differently. Is there any liberal here who'd stay on the same side if an African attacked his mother? Is opinion in U.K. changing now the same way as it is in the U.S.A. over civil rights?" He had studied for three years in Natal. "Maybe I'm a pessimist, but do you really believe that we can all be brothers? I'm a racist. I hate the Afrikaners. Do you really think black and white can love each other?" So far he had been speaking semifacetiously, but there was nothing comic about his last question, "Tell me, would you want to live in Southern Rhodesia?" "No," I said.

Proximity does not always make for friendship. "Most people change from living with them," said another student. "This was the first time I'd ever really lived with Africans and eaten with them. They always eat with their mouths open so you can see what's inside. It's not very pleasant." Here a spectacled student interrupted, "All you can say against them is that they eat with their mouths open. But haven't you met any of the third-year Africans? They're very fine chaps." Yes, they all agreed on this, but the small troubles of living together still caused tension. "I'll tell you one thing that causes unpleasantness. At a dance there may be a European girl sitting on her own at the side. A European gentleman comes up and asks for a dance, and she says no, and he goes away. An African gentleman asks for a dance, and she says no, and you have a racial incident." The young man who said this admitted that there was a shortage of African girls and that generally it was much more difficult for the African than the European students. Yes, they were all agreed, then suddenly a fourth boy said,

"Another thing. When there's a shortage of girls at a dance the Africans dance with one another. Without ulterior motive, I'm sure. And then there's the way they hold hands . . . although maybe to them there's something disgusting about a white boy and a girl holding hands."

A student who had scarcely opened his mouth in these arguments came up to talk to me afterwards. He proved to be a firm but depressed liberal. "This University was a great experiment in multiracialism," he said, "and it's been a colossal flop." When the intellectual cream of the country disliked Africans for their table manners, it seemed pretty hopeless for the less educated majority. The left-wingers from England were the worst. They were the sort who soon turned so fascist they would not allow an African within two feet of them. But whatever the student anxiety about race, there was nothing furtive or hypocritical in their approach; I have seldom heard the problem discussed with such garrulous candor. That in itself is probably a good sign for the future.

There is in Salisbury a core of very hard liberals who are entirely opposed to the principle of white supremacy and who are quite prepared to fight it. For obvious reasons they do not wish to be named. I quote here the composite views of two Salisbury intellectual whites: "The last election was rough, and if they hold another one it will be very tough indeed. The conservatism of the whites is centered on political power and the Land Apportionment Act. They mean to keep both these things, but I don't know whether the whites would really want to get into a fight over Rhodesia. They are brought up in the empirical European way of thinking, in contrast to the Afrikaner, who is not bothered with ideas about political morality. I wonder how the Europeans here would behave after a few farms had been burned, after a few atrocities. I think the farmers would back out. And after all, more than 90 per cent of the Rhodesian whites are living in cities. But a lot of these people feel captured because they've got homes costing £7,000 on which they've already paid £2,000. Most of them have lived very sheltered lives. They haven't learned to boil an egg. If they left Southern Rhodesia, they would find it hard to work."

These liberals singled out for particular odium the self-justificatory arguments of the Right: "Have you ever looked at those letters in the *Rhodesia Herald* giving the argument for white supremacy? They always say two things. First: this is a beautiful country. Second: Rhodesians fought in the Second World War. Now, the first argument is true but irrelevant. The second is not even very true. Most of the war veterans fought in the British Army and came out here afterwards. Most of the Rhodesian troops were black." As I left these two liberal Southern Rhodesians—*New Statesman* readers, without a doubt—one of them called out, "Farewell to this outpost of Empire." The other added in total seriousness, "Let's just hope it stays that way." In Southern Rhodesia it is the left wing that sticks by the Union Jack.

On the way from Salisbury to the Congo I stopped for a few days at Ndola, on the edge of the copper belt in Northern Rhodesia. These were the last days before the country's re-emergence as the new State of Zambia and the portents of coming change were easy to find. At the airports of Lusaka and Ndola, the white officials were training Africans to check the passports, examine the luggage and issue the boarding passes. Both whites and Africans at Ndola airport bar were tolerant of a drunk Cape colored man who had strong views about Zambian independence. Nobody quite understood what these views were. A Welsh post office engineer complained that the other Europeans were slacking out the remaining days of their service, but most seemed to be handing over with good grace. Everyone who spoke of Kenneth Kaunda said something complimentary. The rightists, even more pointedly, said nothing about him at all.

The copper belt was the last outpost of racism. The public houses and restaurants, cinemas, hospitals and schools had been integrated. A few well-to-do Africans had moved and been made welcome in white suburbs. But the white miners, who include many South Africans, guarded the white strongholds of their clubs. In Ndola, most of these had by now admitted some Africans; as independence draws near, it becomes politic to be tolerant.

If Salisbury is Surbiton superimposed on Africa, then the copper belt is its Scunthorpe. On Saturday night, the young men of the town, wearing blue jeans and Beatle haircuts, paraded in front of the cinema queue or sat in the café giving angry stares at the passers-by. They are mostly single and sex-starved. "I'm sick of going to parties here," said a twenty-two-year-old girl from Wales. "It's always four or five girls and forty men. It sounds great, but it's no fun really. They get miserable and fight and the drink runs out." She is a schoolteacher at a primary school here. "My last job was in Birmingham and I didn't like that much. Most of the children in the class were colored, you know. Here there are only two Africans, and the rest are white." Her parents were against her going off to Africa, especially when they discovered how close Ndola was to the Congo. But she and her fellow teachers like it here. They live frugally, even doing their own washing and save anything up to £300 a year. It can get dull—several Ndola whites confessed that they talk to themselves in the mirror—but there are always plenty of serials on the television, indeed, life here is much like northern England: booze, football, gambling, occasional fights. Africa does not seem to impinge. I noticed that almost every car had a fluffy animal hanging in front of the windscreen as a mascot. These were tigers, kangaroos and koala bears—animals that are not found in Africa.

Thanks to the books by the Reverend Colin Morris, the Western public has heard of the good work done by some of the churches in the copper belt. In the fine tradition of Livingstone, they campaigned against the different kinds of color bar imposed by the European miners. There was even a color bar in some of the churches themselves. Today this would be unthinkable. All races come, for example, to St. Andrew's Church in the mainly white district of Ndola. The minister, David Stivens, the son of the parish priest of the island of Iona, went from Oxford to Canada, where he worked many years in a lumber company before taking holy orders. He and his wife had learned Portuguese in preparation for taking a church in Angola, but were at the last moment refused permission to enter the country. St. Andrew's is his first church. Having read Morris's books beforehand, he was surprised by what he found. "Things have happened so quickly it isn't funny. When I first came here, I was influenced by Morris's writing. Then I said, 'Where is it [the color bar]? We've been misled.' But everyone told me it had been just as Morris had described it a few years before. To take one example: A boss of mine came out here several years ago and shook hands with my African clerk, and people had goose pimples. Two years ago he came out and shook hands with my African clerk, and nobody thought anything about it. This year he came out and shook hands with my African clerk, and if he hadn't it would have been considered a grave discourtesy." Only five years ago, he said, there were people who walked out of a church if an African came in. "Now there are two hundred Africans living in the European area. We try to make this church a home to Africans, but it's terribly difficult. The District Church Council here doesn't want the educated Africans to go to St. Andrew's because it skims the cream off the top . . . It used to be the case that an African would find it awkward to come to the church. Now the boot is on the other foot. We find it awkward that they don't come."

The minister pointed out several members of his congregation as they left the church: "I'll tell you one very interesting thing here. Practically all the Government administration are active churchgoers and social workers. I've knocked about a bit, but I don't think I know anywhere in the world where the top boys in Government are such churchgoers and who find that the Church has some answers to their problems." Although a Scot in the United Church of Central Africa, Mr. Stivens is not opposed to the Northern Rhodesian practice of playing games on Sundays. The Anglicans and Roman Catholics actively support it, while about half Mr. Stivens's fellow noncomformists are anti-Sabbatarian. He is, however, worried by the difficulty of organizing a youth club in the copper belt.

Mr. Stivens remains impressed by the way that Europeans in the copper belt have reacted to the approach of Zambia. He showed me the thoughts he had written about this matter in a church magazine. "People have constantly implied that life in the copper belt is superficial (at least for Europeans). I question this. Rather would I say that the superficial appearance of the life of so many derives from torn and tormented souls—that these folk are living from perhaps a deeper level than any I have ever met. We Canadians, on the whole, are so secure and set in our ways. Had we in Canada been asked to make the psychological and spiritual adjustment which has been demanded of the folk here over the past five or ten years, we would all be psychopaths. There are very few here who think and even pray the same as they could have and would have one half decade ago. Oh, for a good, wholesome Canadian rut?"

St. Andrew's Church in Ndola had one sad week of fame when it appeared on the television screens of the world. It was here that the body of Dag Hammarskjöld lay in state after being found among the wreckage of his airplane. There is a sports stadium in Ndola which has been named after him; it would be pleasant to feel that here, so near to the Congo, he was remembered with pride and respect. In fact most of the whites still recall him with loathing. "We are proud that he should have died in Ndola," said one notorious U.N.-hater, "but ashamed that it wasn't actually one of our blokes that filled him in."

The most apt epitaph for the Swede comes from the greatest of all white men in Africa:

"All I can add in my solitude, is, may Heaven's rich blessing come down on everyone, American, English, or Turk, who will help heal this open sore of the world."

These were the last written words of David Livingstone, who died, at Chitambo's Village not far away on May 1, 1873.

South Africa

"I HAD to go up to the airport to meet a friend who was visiting South Africa for the first time and had just come in from Lagos. As soon as he left the airport he said he could feel that this was a country with stability, where people are here to stay. I thought it was extraordinarily sensitive of him to notice this right away." The speaker, needless to say, was a South African, and the remark was promptly capped by another in the group: "A friend of mine came into this country from the north and immediately said what a change it was to see happy Africans."

The South Africans constantly say how much they resent foreigners who make uninformed, snap judgments about their country. This is not true. They welcome any judgment, however uninformed and snap, provided it is favorable. No people in the world is so susceptible to the flattery of strangers. The two South Africans whom I have just quoted were obviously hoping that I would chip in with some equally friendly impression of Johannesburg. It would not have been honest to do so. The first impressions were of: an airport Inquiries desk which, when asked how to find a suburban address, answered, "That's a bleddy silly question"; the conductor of the airport bus who deliberately, and sneeringly, gave £5 worth of change in silver; the racial segregation of public lavatories, park benches, and lifts; the hotel desk porter who said insolently and incorrectly, "You left your key up in your room, man. You'd better go up and fetch it"; the airline office which lost and has not yet found my mail for the last month; the dank bars for (white) men only; the piano-infested hotel lounges; a cinema whose ceiling and walls are decorated to give the impression of sitting outdoors at night in Disney's medieval Germany under twinkling stars, surrounded by gabled houses and castles, also with lights in their latticed windows. These were some of the things I noticed during the first hours in Johannesburg. I wrote in my diary, "Manchester under Fascism." It was a spurious judgment, for Jo'burg is comparable to no other city, while Dr. Verwoerd's régime is not, yet, fascist.

The three million white people in South Africa own seven eighths of its land and outnumber the whites in the rest of "black" Africa by over five to one. It is the only nation on the continent with any claim to being a white state. It would therefore be an impertinence to try to describe in any detail the whites of South Africa. There have been more than enough attempts by other hands. Moreover, I am concerned in this book more with the whites as minorities within black states than with the special case of a white state largely cut off—by apartheid

—from the surrounding natives. Indeed, the Nationalists claim that the Dutch occupied most of what is now the Republic even before the Bantu arrived, and that therefore they, the whites, are really the natives. But some remarks on the South African whites are necessary, if only because they exert such fascination and influence on white people throughout the rest of the continent. The Republic, as it is always called, is even more discussed and misunderstood in Leopoldville or Dar es Salaam than in London. The white Kenyans (quite apart from Afrikaners living there) constantly debate whether to move to South Africa. A very large number object to Verwoerd's racial policy, while the more right-wing ones doubt whether "the whites will really make a stand of it."

The problem of South Africa, to the South African whites themselves, does not even refer to apartheid. They are far more concerned with the tension between the 1,200,000 English- and the 1,800,000 Afrikaans-speaking whites. The acceleration of apartheid and the creation of Bantustans mean that white people have less and less contact with blacks, and scarcely even see them at night in the cities. Ten years ago, whites in Johannesburg lived in terror of black gangsters. These gangsters are now obliged to operate only in African townships. In *The Condition of the Working Class in England*, Friedrich Engels described how Manchester was designed so that the bourgeoisie were spared the sight of the proletarian cottages hidden between the arterial roads to the suburbs. In Johannesburg the position is reversed. The whites live in the city itself, while the blacks commute from the suburbs to the commercial center.

If the average white South African finds the apartheid question remote, he is constantly aware of the language problem. Although most Afrikaners speak some English, few of the newer arrivals speak Afrikaans or even try to learn it. The language question affects education, legal proceedings, broadcasting, cinemas and the home. Quarrels about which language to use are a frequent touch-point of quarrel in mixed English-Afrikaner marriages. Even in peaceful Switzerland, which has been federated for five hundred years, the French-speaking and German-speaking communities are mutually hostile, although there they live in clearly divided parts of the country. It is far worse in South Africa, where a big Afrikaner minority lives in Natal and almost as many English in Transvaal. When one remembers that English and Afrikaners fought a civil war here only sixty years ago, it is hardly surprising that South Africa's two political parties divide mainly on language lines. In many smaller towns the English and Afrikaners live in clearly separated districts. The English call the Afrikaners "hairies," who in turn call the English "red necks." Insofar as South Africans worry about apartheid, it is mostly in terms of the language questions. Most English-speaking United Party supporters are in favor of white supremacy and object only to Dr. Verwoerd's tactless and doctrinaire methods. The Afrikaans-speaking Nationalist Party supporters often equate liberal and outside criticism with old English imperialism. Certainly there is a streak of racism in English attitudes to the Afrikaner, or Boer. It is similar to the anti-German racism which infects both the right and left wings of British public opinion. Cartoons of the Boer leaders in Conservative newspapers in 1900 are remarkably like the cartoons of Boer leaders in the *New Statesman* today: thick necks, square heads, piggy faces.

In fact, many foreign visitors—and I was one—are surprised to find themselves feeling respect and admiration for the Afrikaners. The great majority of them are small farmers, virtually peasants, with fifty acres or so for dairy farming, maize, and perhaps a little tobacco. I visited several farms round Randfontein, among rolling veldt which in winter glows purple, cream and chocolate. At the first farm I made the mistake of asking the son of the house, "How many Africans do you employ?" Fortunately, he misunderstood and replied, "Yes, we're Africans." Later he explained that the farm employed two *naturelle*.

The family had lived for five generations in a house whose walls and roof were made from corrugated iron. Most of the family now live in Johannesburg, because there is not enough work or wealth on the farm. These Afrikaners still cling to ancient methods and customs of agriculture. At another farm I asked Mr. Douw Van der Welt how a farmer divided his property up among his sons. The old man grinned and started to trace a plan of a farm in the dust with his stick. He divided the plan up into four equal parts for four sons. "But," he said, tracing a swirl in the neat plan, "if there's a peach tree in one strip but not in the next, they move the line round to include the tree. *In ondre vorts*," he concluded in half Afrikaans, "there's a fokk oop." They have the natural dignity and hospitality of the real farmer. At another farm Petrus Jacobus Van Wyk, aged sixty, and with a bad leg, smilingly showed us round his geese, chickens, vegetables and the outdoor stove for baking biscuits. He attends the strictest sect of the Dutch Reformed Church, has never taken a holiday, but occasionally meets up with his relatives for a party. Although British journalists are anathema to the Nationalists, I met nothing but courtesy from the Afrikaners.

A Welshman who had left South Africa for Northern Rhodesia was one of many who moaned that the Afrikaners were still fighting the Boer War: "They're obsessed with it, but of course it's the only war they've got. We've had so many. I mean the Yanks, the French, the Germans. You name them, we've fought them." I visited one farm where the original house was burned down by the British. The owner had built the charred doorposts into the new house which is still standing. "The British were naughty," said Mrs. M. Mulder, the widow who lives there now, but this was the extent of Boer War animosity that I heard. A South African liberal said half in joke, "As soon as the Nationalists came to power after the Second World War, they reckoned that they'd finally won the Boer War and therefore could stop worrying about it." I suspect that the English in South Africa, and in Rhodesia for that matter, have a different motive for their dislike of the Afrikaner and the obsession with the Boer War. They are themselves haunted by the idea that they are johnnies-come-lately to Africa, that they do not really belong. They are therefore jealous of the Afrikaners whose history on the continent goes back through the Boer War and the Great Trek to the seventeenth century. The Southern Rhodesians have tried to create their own myth of the pioneer to rival that of the Boers. But it does not really convince. In the first place, half Rhodes's pioneers were Afrikaners. In the second place, it is evident that the overwhelming majority of Southern Rhodesians are newcomers or first-generation settlers.

It is partly because the Boers think themselves Africans that they maintain such a strange attitude to the blacks. In fact, many of them are partly black, and an awareness of this explains the pedantic lunacy of the apartheid laws. There was so much miscegenation in the early days of the colony that many Afrikaners are actually darker-skinned than the people legally classified as "coloreds." One day in the Newlands suburb of Johannesburg I talked to an Asian shopkeeper who has been moved to a home in a distant township and forbidden to sleep in the shop which his family has owned for generations. I walked farther down the street to the next shop, owned by a man of still darker skin, whom I guessed to either be Asian or Cape colored. "How's business?" I asked and was astonished by his reply. "This is a white district, but on every corner you've got a bloody Chinaman or an Indian. Don't you look on the bad things, man. You go and see what they're doing for the coloreds. Better houses than the whites have got, man." There are several prominent Afrikaner politicans who look almost mulatto.

The terror of interbreeding goes with the Afrikaner's curious sexual attitude to the blacks. It was they, more than the English, who wanted the law against interracial sex. It is generally they who break the same law. This secret and guilty lust helps to explain the popularity of Lourenço Marques, in nearby Mozambique, as a South African holiday resort. The native brothels there are open to customers of all races and they attract many Afrikaners. For this reason "L.M." has the same scandalous sound to white South Africans that Paris had to Victorian Englishmen.

Afrikaner attitudes to the native range from old-style paternalism to literal apartheid. A tobacco farmer, C. P. Peach, expressed the traditional view well: "You need to employ labor if you have tobacco. And it's cheaper to keep them all the year round than to hire them when you need them. Mind you, we pay them well—three or four shillings a day, which is good money. And on top of this we feed them. And, of course, you can't have your natives going around in rags. You've got to have them well dressed in case you have visitors. Otherwise people would go away saying, 'Look, his natives are practically naked.' " But the new-style Nationalist wants the complete separation of the races, with the blacks living in semiautonomous Bantustans. Carried to its logical conclusion, this means that whites should not employ black labor. Indeed, one Afrikaner teachers' training college recently decreed that students would make their own beds and clean their own rooms so as not to employ Bantus. (This high-minded plan broke down after a few months because the students found that housework interfered with their studies.) The foreign press often makes out that the extreme Nationalists are fanatic "nigger-haters." On the contrary, it is the doctrinaire extremists who are most meticulous in demanding respect for the blacks. One road sign near Johannesburg has been changed in recent years from "Beware: Natives Crossing" to "Caution: Natives Crossing" to "Please Slow Down: Bantu Crossing."

It was the previous generation of Nationalist politicians who proclaimed the inferiority of the blacks. The present leaders, under Dr. Verwoerd, are at once more extreme and more liberal. They believe in what they call "separate development" for whites and blacks, but they do not, in theory, consider the Bantus an inferior race, merely one at a lower stage of development. The South African Bureau of Racial Affairs, the ideological mouthpiece of the Nationalist Party, has stressed the need for South Africa to get on well with independent African countries. The Nationalist-leaning weekly magazine *Newscheck*, a kind of *Time* for all African affairs, is scrupulously fair and accurate about events north of the Limpopo.

These apparently temperate policies of the régime are based on a bedrock of fanaticism. Most members of the Cabinet, including Dr. Verwoerd, are members of the

Broederbond Society, a kind of cross between the IRA and Mau Mau. Joining members have to sense magic rites conducted in pitch darkness, followed by fearsome oaths. The society is dedicated to the triumph of Afrikanerdom and considers itself accountable only to God. It used to take inspiration from Hitler's National Socialist Party, but now gets its guidance from the Dutch Reformed Church (or Dutch Deformed, as the English South Africans call it). The character of this faith is splendidly illustrated in the sermon preached by the Reverend G. J. J. Boshoff on the day after the shooting of Dr. Verwoerd in 1960. It has been quoted before, but is well worth quoting again:

The wounding of Dr. Verwoerd on the eve of our Day of Humiliation has made big tears fall on our altar. Nobody will tell the Afrikaner what he is to say at the altar . . . the Afrikaner's altar is his biggest weapon, his nuclear bomb, his firing squad. For three centuries the history of the Afrikaner people has been one long *via dolorosa*. There is nothing that the enemy fears so much as an Afrikaner who prays. The black giant of Africa is eating bread for which he has not sweated, he wants to wear clothes that do not fit him, he wants to pay with what he does not yet have, distribute what he does not yet possess, wants to talk about things he does not yet understand, wants to be where he still is not. By contrast, the white giant is entirely ignored. The real giant of Africa, the white man—and his name is Afrikaner—does not come into the picture at all.

And so on. That is the real spirit of Afrikanerdom: hard, antique, mysterious, almost mystical.

This may be the soul of the Afrikaner. But the outward man is often surprisingly different. Most British people have an idea of Dr. Verwoerd himself as a dour, scowling fanatic, yet nothing could be farther from the truth. A passionate liberal South African once remarked to me, "Verwoerd is a brilliant speaker, very moderate and fatherly and persuasive. I don't know whether you've heard him on the radio or seen him on TV, but you listen to him and think, 'Well, he's right.' Only afterwards do you realize that he's hoodwinked you."

Leaving ethics aside, there is one serious flaw in the idea of separate development: it is entirely unworkable. The whites, who own seven eighths of the land and all the mineral and industrial wealth, cannot survive without African labor. The eleven million Africans, even when finally herded into their self-governing Bantustans, could not survive without white capital. Separate development could work only if the Africans took three quarters of the economic wealth of the country and left the whites to independence on a small "Blankustan." It is not an idea that would appeal to the mass of the white population.

If separate development is ridiculous, it is far less so when proposed by the Nationalist Afrikaners. Most of their supporters are workers and small farmers who genuinely could do without black labor. They can, and loudly do, claim that the English-speaking United Party is hypocritical in its attitude to the blacks, wanting to keep black labor without allowing them any increase in political development. Many United Party supporters seem guiltily aware of this. They are much more confused and neurotic about the future than are the Afrikaners themselves. They are particularly hostile and jumpy in their attitude to foreigners and to what "the world thinks of South Africa." Here, for example, is the résumé of a conversation at dinner between my host, who is a lawyer, his wife, and an anthropologist guest.

It began with some pointed anecdotes about foreign journalists in South Africa: "Did you hear about the Danish woman reporter who had been looking round an African township and ended up at the children's crèche? Just as she was about to leave she asked if it was allowed to give one of the children a banana. She pushed the banana through the side of the playpen, and just at this moment the photographer took a picture which appeared in the newspaper under the heading: OUR REPORTER FEEDS STARVING AFRICAN CHILDREN IN CONCENTRATION CAMP. Then there was an English reporter who was shown round a township, and at the end he told his guide 'Yes, it's very impressive. But unfortunately I'm not allowed to say so, as I've been told to write unfavorable articles.' There was another Dane who was absolutely amazed to see a host of green buses for Africans at a works exit. 'Do you mean you don't make them walk to work?' he asked." Stories like this are part of the folk legend of modern South Africa and Southern Rhodesia. Probably most of them have some basis in fact, although with a very different point. For instance, many journalists have written about African buses recently—not to express surprise that such things should exist, but to protest against the high fares demanded between the place of work and the distant townships.

After this warming-up, the anthropologist went into a long dissertation about various African tribes which, since it was not of any intrinsic interest, can have been designed only to show a foreigner, first, how complicated the African question is, second, how much interest the whites take in the black, third, how African living standards are continually rising. The lawyer went as far as to "say one thing for the Nationalists. They've done more for the African than we ever did. I know an Englishman in North Transvaal who hates this Government just because it's doing too much for the blacks in terms of medicine and social services. He says we should be keeping their numbers down." This United Party supporter then went on to attack the natives because they did not like to mix with other tribes in a township: "That's a basic defect in the African character. You can't imagine a Syrian or a Swede or a Spaniard complaining about his next-door neighbor but one." (This seemed to me a curious remark from a South African.)

As the evening went on the three waxed more and more indignant against liberals and foreigners, until it was all I could do to keep silent. But once it became clear that I did not want to argue the conversation suddenly went into reverse. The anthropologist began to deplore the fact that Africans were obliged to live apart from their families, that they weren't allowed homes, even slums, in the big cities. The hostess ended the evening by saying that very probably Africans would be happier starving in a state of their own, like Ghana, rather than being told how to live, however comfortably, by Europeans. The other two sadly agreed with her.

By some psychological quirk, many white South Africans often comfort themselves with foolish foreign criticism. Every time some ignorant Englishman says that the South African natives are starving, or that the courts are rigged, these South Africans can divert their own guilt into resentment against outsiders. A man who knows himself guilty of theft is glad to be falsely accused of wife-beating. The Swedes, above all, serve as a satisfying bogy-figure of prejudiced, ignorant interference. One story is told of a conference where the Swedish delegation announced at dinner, "Before coming here, we had been a hundred per cent against apartheid. We are now a hundred and twenty per cent against, and we think your country stinks." Several South Africans told me that they now refused to buy Swedish motorcars, although, as it happened, none had ever owned one before. The English-speaking South Africans, who feel an attachment to Europe, seem far more annoyed than the Afrikaners by the anti-South Africa propaganda from abroad.

South Africans constantly say that it is quite impossible to take any attitude to their country until one has lived there several years. On the other hand, they themselves pass emphatic judgments on countries like Ghana, Tanganyika and Soviet Russia which they have not visited at all. I once listened patiently for half an hour to a lady of wildly bigoted views: any article by a Negro was immediately published in *The New Yorker;* South Africa was so peaceful that she could drive a car alone for as much as twelve miles. And so on. She then turned the conversation to her native Yugoslavia, which she had seen for the last time in 1945. She said that the country was supported entirely by U.S. aid, that half the population was starving, and much besides. I explained to her as politely as possible that, having visited Yugoslavia many times and spent as much as eighteen months in the country, I thought she had exaggerated. "But of course you didn't understand," she replied complacently; "you are not a Yugoslav."

The great majority of recent British immigrants settle down easily in South Africa. Although the South Africans offer a free flight to a prospective immigrant and his family, they have had few bad debts in the form of people coming out for the ride and then returning to Britain. Many newcomers live in a few big blocks of flats in the Berea area of Johannesburg. Maracynth flats, for example, are almost entirely filled by British immigrants like Mrs. Ellie Woods from Glasgow: "My husband used to work for a locomotive firm, but he became redundant. So he and a friend came over for £25 each to have a look. The kids and I came over free. He's got a good job now, but it's quite expensive here. I used to pay £9 a month for a flat, but here it's £20, and it's the cheapest flat in the block. There are seven Scots couples living here and we go around together. I miss home, of course. And the TV. I didn't miss it at first when the country was new and there were lots of new things to see . . . Yes, I have help. We have a flat boy who comes in to do the polishing and a girl who comes and does some of the washing. The maid gets £7 a month and works from 7:30 till 5 and Saturday mornings . . . Things aren't as bad here as people say back home. Occasionally the native girls get knifed, but that's really nothing to do with you."

In spite of South Africa's ever-expanding wealth, there are many poor whites in the cities. Indeed, there are more white beggars than black in central Johannesburg. The Mayfair, Newlands and Brixton districts of Johannesburg are comparable to the blight areas of Manchester or South London. "There's a lot of unemployment here," said a Brixton man, who was leaning on his garden wall reading a Western. "It's all these foreigners coming in. You can see hundreds of people outside the employment exchange each day." These foreigners are mostly English, German and Dutch who have moved in to replace the Indians, forced out by the apartheid laws on residence. Johannesburg's Brixton is rather like ours, except that one doesn't see so many black faces.

A former steeplejack, like the tramp from Pinter's *Caretaker*, took me into his dingy cottage and complained about his pension: "I think it's a shame on a nation. I think sooner or later God won't stand for it. I've done my bit for the country—its all in the records in Pretoria—secret service, intelligence and the rest of it . . . Take up your cross and bear it, that's the real Christian . . . I used to be one of the leading pigeon fanciers in Johannesburg, but I had to give away all my pigeons for the sake of the country." Like everyone I spoke to in this district, he is a Nationalist. "The Nationalists do a lot for the people, both for the English and the Afrikaner. Look at the welfare, for example. Even for tramps they do things. The others, the Smuts party, they're all right for the rich people who want to meet each other at barbecues, but for the poorer people they don't do anything."

Outside South Africa it is the Communists and Socialists who are loudest against apartheid. Inside South Africa it is the working-class whites who keep the system in power. The only left-wing M.P. in South Africa, Helen Suzman of the Progressive Party, represents the richest constituency in the country, the Houghton suburb of Johannesburg, where the successful business and professional people aspire to live. Many of them are Jews. Indeed, many of the names of people arrested or held under the ninety-day system for anti-Government agitation are Jewish. The Jews of the Transvaal can be proud of their role in South Africa. Many of them have grown rich in the mining rush of the last eighty years, but they have not sold out their principles. During the early years of the Hitler régime the Nationalists turned anti-Semitic, but this was soon dropped after the defeat of Germany. After 1948, when the Nationalists won power, they wooed the support of the Jewish community. The SABRA and other organs of Afrikaner thinking often compared the position of South Africa with that of Israel surrounded by hostile Arabs. But the majority of South African Jews have been resolutely opposed to apartheid. The breach became even more clear when Israel cast its vote against South Africa in the United Nations. Israeli diplomats in South Africa have sometimes insisted on traveling in Asian rather than white buses. Many Zionists among the Jewish community have returned to Israel, but the great majority remain, unhappily, put. One Jewish liberal told me, "A lot of my generation, the young marrieds, and especially the Jewish community, are very restless. A lot of them go to London, but South Africans are not often happy in London. You feel it immediately—a kind of claustrophobia. We're used to space in this country."

The South Africans often complain that they are misunderstood abroad. In one important respect this is true. The average liberal-minded Englishman, who is rightly opposed to apartheid, wrongly imagines that the voice of protest is not heard in South Africa itself. I confess that before going there I had imagined, first, that justice was entirely under the control of the police; second, that public protest against apartheid was suppressed; third, that the white opposition to racism was confined to a handful of liberals, most of them living in exile. All these assumptions, which I would bet are shared by many English people, are grotesquely incorrect.

The laws of South Africa may be odious, but the law men have not yet been corrupted. There could be no better example of this than the Rivonia trial last year of Nelson Mandela and others, both white and black, who had conspired to use violence against the state. Outside liberal opinion presented the trial as a conspiracy against freedom. Yet liberals inside South Africa regarded it as a victory. Many of them no doubt agree with Mandela that the time has come to use violence as well as agitation to overthrow the régime, but they were not shocked by the sentences. One liberal summed up his feelings: "There was no doubt that the plotters were guilty. In fact, what really annoyed us about the case was the way they allowed themselves to get caught red-handed and all in a bunch. What really surprised us was the judge, who's a fanatical Nat, and was appointed only recently by Verwoerd. On the first day of the trial, the prosecuting counsel made a speech in which he kept referring to the accused men as the guilty men. The judge came down on him like a stone and said he wasn't to use that kind of talk in his court . . . It was a scrupulously fair trial."

The English-language South African press is, to my mind, the finest in the world. Their circulation is small; the leading *Rand Daily Mail* sells only eighty thousand. Much of their contents is as provincial as you would find in newspapers published from Bradford or Newcastle. What distinguishes them is persistent and fearless reporting of the inhumanities of the régime, together with fierce and reasoned editorial opposition. The régime has passed laws making it possible to suppress the press almost overnight. So far it has not used these extreme measures, although all newspapers are hampered by minor censorship, such as a rule forbidding them to quote any statement by political detainees. It should be added that some of the Afrikaner Nationalist newspapers have been scrupulous in defense of free expression. Indeed, those who know Afrikaans say that the *Burger* of Cape Town is honest by any standards.

The credit for press freedom goes less to Dr. Verwoerd than to the hundreds of journalists who have refused to budge under pressure. The editor of the *Rand Daily Mail,* Laurence Gandar, is a man of such steadfast courage and honesty that to read his admirable newspaper each day revives a long-faded pride in the profession of journalism. Life is not easy for journalists. Most of them are automatically suspect to the police. Names of reporters are found in almost every list of people held under the ninety-day law. I chanced to be drinking in one of Johannesburg's newspaper public houses when the news broke of a mass raid. An excited reporter burst in to tell his colleagues, "It's happened. They took A and B and that fellow C in Cape Town." "Not A? It's fantastic. He'd never be mixed up with sabotage," somebody said. A man recently out from England said to me, "I'm getting out of this game, mate. The newspaper business is becoming impossible here." Like the rest of them, he is still there. These journalists give full coverage to the arrests. A woman reporter whose home was searched wrote up a front-page account of the incident and her children's terror. The fortitude of these journalists is all the more remarkable because they are poorly paid by any standards. It would be pleasant to think that the British press would prove as incorruptible under circumstances as bad. I doubt it. Some months before going to South Africa I had been talking with a group of journalists in a Fleet Street pub. One of them, who had just come back from South Africa, said that the South African press was more free than ours. The company laughed it off as the attempt of a right-wing man to be shocking. Unfortunately he was telling the literal truth. There are more English-language papers in London than South Africa in which the truth is bent.

The liberal opposition to Dr. Verwoerd's racial policies is both bigger and tougher than is assumed outside. About 7 per cent of the electorate voted in 1961 for the Progressive or Liberal parties. This proportion, although apparently small, included a good part of the lawyers, doctors, teachers, students, journalists, and a considerable number of English-speaking businessmen. The multimillionaire, Harry Oppenheimer, is the financial backer of the Progressive Party. Most of the liberals come from the big cities, and they are often the people that foreigners meet because they themselves are internationally minded. It is easy, indeed dangerously easy, to enter a social set in which everybody is against the régime. This produces a quite unjustified sense of optimism about the future.

The kind of South African who votes for the United Party is eager to tell you that his is not a police state. Maybe. It is, however, the only English-speaking country to which I have been where people habitually lower their voices when talking politics in a public place. Over morning coffee one day at a flat in the Hillbrow district of Johannesburg there came a loud bang on the door.

"Pack your bags for ninety days," somebody joked, but nobody laughed. The joke has been made too often before, and it conceals a real fear. Most of the liberals are of English or Jewish origin, but there is also a hard core of rebel Afrikaners. These men and women have had to defy not only the Government but also the force of their own upbringing and legend. Consequently, they are hard, fanatical, and unbreakable.

The tragedy of South Africa is the suppression of its blacks. At the same time, it is a tragedy for the whites; and I do not intend by this just the usual sanctimonious platitude. For instance, the fate of the whites in Southern Rhodesia is not tragic, merely uncomfortable. Most of them are recent arrivals who do not truly belong in Africa, have no national feeling or character, and remain mostly for economic reasons. It would be uncomfortable for them to have to move elsewhere, but not, surely, a tragedy. The South Africans, on the other hand, do belong in Africa. Theirs is a vital, imaginative nation with a strong culture and character of its own. It is typical of this culture and character to have produced a political system so extreme, wrong and visionary as "separate development," and also such a vigorous opposition.

South Africans can be cruel on a gigantic scale, but they are seldom petty or mean. They are violent and extravagant both in principle and in pleasure. My Afrikaner taxi driver, on the way out to the airport, told me a story of what had happened after the races the previous week: "I had one man as a fare—I'd known him a long time from the race track—who'd won a packet on the July handicap. So I took him along to one of the clubs, where he found a woman. Then he said he wanted a Durban woman. So I took him to Durban, and he found a woman. Then he said he wanted to buy her a fur coat, so we went to Cape Town . . ."

Portuguese Territories

"FIRST IN, LAST OUT" might almost serve as a motto for the Portuguese in Africa, except that they do not intend to get out at all. They settled in the Canary Islands in 1424, reached the Rio de Oro in 1436, Cape Blanco in 1441, Cape Verde in 1446, and Sierra Leone by 1460, the year of the death of Henry the Navigator, who planned and directed these expeditions. By 1483 they had reached the Congo, by 1487 they were round the Cape of Good Hope, and by the end of the fifteenth century reached India by sea. Captain Diogo Cao, Bartolomeu Dias and Vasco da Gama . . . their names still ring heroic. They were as steadfast in settlement as in discovery. To the entire coast, but particularly to the shores of Mozambique and Angola, came knights in metal breastplates and plumed helmets, Jesuits aflame with the fanaticism of the young order, and plenipotentiaries of a tiny kingdom that yet controlled almost a fifth of the known world. They built cities and churches, they rode on punitive wars into the jungle, and they died in droves at the start of each rainy season.

One century of glory was followed by four of torpor. The civilizing mission, so often proclaimed in the fifteenth and sixteenth centuries, petered out in apathy. The colonial governors were content with a small strip of Portuguese territory on the coast; the priests gave up any attempt at turning Africans into Christians; Church, State and the merchants joined in the single-minded plunder of Africa for ivory, gold and, above all, slaves. The Portuguese carried at least three million slaves from Angola alone to the plantations of the Americas. Many more millions died on the journey. About 25,000 slaves a year were carried from Mozambique as late as 1850. Black Mother, as they called Central Africa, was plundered of human beings by Portuguese, Arabs, Dutch, French and British. No wonder the Black Mother has lost weight. Angola on the west coast is one of the world's most underpopulated countries. In its 481,352 square miles there are 4,500,000 Africans, less than 300,000 Europeans and 50,000 mulattoes. Mozambique, which stretches along the east coast between South Africa and Tanganyika, has 6,200,000 Africans and a white population estimated at 110,000.

If the Portuguese had been more energetic during the last century, they might have joined up their two Central African territories to include what are now the Rhodesias. But Lisbon's attitude to these colonies remained lethargic until this century, when foreign criticism provoked a number of contradictory reforms. At the same time, the Portuguese discovered new possibilities of wealth to replace the forbidden slave trade. The diamonds and coffee of Angola made the colony into a gain instead of a loss. The rise of African nationalism and the Angolan uprising of 1961 actually prodded the Portuguese into energetic action. They abolished forced labor by law, although not always in fact, built roads, bridges, and airstrips throughout the territories as a strategic help to the military; they turned the colonies into provinces of Portugal and the Africans into Portuguese citizens. Everyone—white, black or mulatto—in Mozambique and Angola now enjoys the same political rights as the metropolitan Portuguese: that is, very few.

Even before going to Portuguese Africa, I was subjected to the gentle and courteous propaganda about Portugal's historic mission. Their Consul-General in Johannesburg, Dr. Pedro Pinto, has a charming line in Portuguese blarney. (If there is no Portuguese word for blarney, there should be.) "We would like to see a policy of assimilation everywhere between Mozambique and Angola. This would be a barrier between the black racial hatred from the north and the—how shall I say—exaggerated white policy of South Africa." He praised the mixing of black and white children in schools, and of black and white grownups in bed. "None of the Portuguese in Africa are really pure Portuguese. Even in Lisbon if you go on a tram you see few really Portuguese faces. You see Oriental eyes, Negroid shoulders . . . Assimilation has increased in Angola since the Portuguese troops went there. There have been many African babies recently with long Portuguese noses." Dr.

Pinto was delighted with the sudden signs of tolerance shown towards Portugal by Malawi. He pointed to the map of Mozambique: "Anyone who holds this part of the coast controls the hinterland. It's the only outlet for Northern Rhodesia [now Zambia]and Malawi. That's why Dr. Banda is so friendly towards us nowadays. It's not because he loves our beautiful eyes." Like so many Portuguese, Dr. Pinto talked of making a Brazil in Africa—racially mixed but guided by Lusitanian culture. He is fond of African art and, shortly before I left, showed me a book of carvings, published in the United States. "Do you see this?" he asked, indicating a West African statuette of a man in cocked hat and ballooned breeches. "The author says this is an ancestral African figure. But it is sixteenth-century Portuguese, you see."

I went first to Lourenço Marques, the capital of Mozambique, and certainly one of the pleasantest cities in Africa—for the whites, at any rate. After the frost of Johannesburg, it was good to come to the warmth of the Indian Ocean. But the change was more than physical. It was like coming from Manchester to the Mediterranean. People seemed to be laughing, talking loudly and enjoying themselves. A woman and four children rode with me in a miniature bus to the hotel, the woman sitting up next to the black driver while the children screamed with excitement and climbed over the seats. The smallest girl offered sweets round, and all four crossed themselves when the bus went past a cemetery. No sooner done, than they once more burst out laughing.

The white part of the city lies along broad avenues

parallel to the coast. From your villa or flat you look out over palm trees to the ocean and a series of low-lying islands in the distance. There are plenty of bright outdoor cafés where you can chatter, drink coffee, and get your shoes shined. The food is famous throughout southern Africa: prawn or chicken *piri-piri*—a kind of pimento, lobsters, green wine from the home country. There are bullfights several times a year, with bulls brought by ship from Lisbon, and moderately saucy nightclubs for those who prefer gentler sport. It is a city of style and beauty. The new National Bank's offices have been decorated with a mosaic a hundred feet long, there is a new church in the shape of a paper hat, and even the headquarters of the PIDE, secret police, is fronted with blue and white glazed porcelain panels showing fisherfolk at work and play.

There are many houses in Lourenço Marques with tall chimneys like bottles. These are characteristic of Pancho Geddes, a young Portuguese architect who studied in South Africa. An admirer of Gaudi, he experiments with "a vernacular style of architecture which people can do themselves with sticks and thatch and blockhauling." He showed us one of his new blocks of flats called "the smiling lion," after a decorating motif. "It's a patterning that starts off from a primitive theme. It's very colorful, with very bold, very strong forms of decoration which people who are not Europeans can command." He showed us the plans of a house composed mostly of bottle shapes, tiered bosoms on totem poles, and assorted breast symbols: "This is the plan for a house on a *kopje*. It's going to be called 'The Habitable Woman.'" His house is filled with wood carvings in which long tubers rise up like antennae from the central block of the trunk. A man of varied enthusiasms, Mr. Geddes was also busy with founding a multiracial boarding school in Swaziland and with publishing a pre- and postnatal handbook for African women.

South Africans and Southern Rhodesians troop to Mozambique on holiday. "Of course, it wouldn't seem much to you," they often said, "but for us it seems marvelously continental." They used the word "continental" in just the same way as the English do, meaning Latin—warm, spicy, relaxed, and erotic. Lourenço Marques is the only town I have been to in Africa that really seems like Europe. The South Africans on holiday wear the same kind of awkward, bemused look as the English on holiday in Spain: the men in blazers and flannels, the women in headscarves and sun-red necks; the jokes about garlic and "Mozambique belly"; the prevailing sense of naughtiness. The big Polana Hotel is more than half filled with rich Johannesburg Jews who keep a reserved distance from the rich Gentile drinking set of the Yacht Club. The Southern Rhodesians go rather to Beira up the coast, which they have turned into a kind of hot Blackpool. The youngsters in the evening descend on the cafés and soon get drunk on the unaccustomed wine. Three teenage girls in jeans swayed arm-in-arm round a quiet Beira square, to yell at the Portuguese men in their outdoor cafés, "Don't you stare at me!" They were joined by two white-faced young men wearing cowboy hats. From a quiet *cervejeria* down the street came the disjointed chorus of "Over the Sea to Skye" and, later still, of "Onward Christian Soldiers."

The charm of "L.M." is matched by the friendliness of the Portuguese officials. They are humorous, self-deprecating, and sweetly reasonable. "Frankly," says one, "it's not the left-wingers and African Nationalists I'm afraid of. It's the right-wing Europeans. Some of these people are just looking for an excuse to massacre the blacks as they did in Angola." Another says, "I believe that this is the only place in Africa where you can see Europeans working the soil with their hands, perhaps in even worse conditions than the blacks. We give farms to white and blacks regardless of color on the Government settlement schemes . . . If we believe in Western civilization and in Christianity, that is to say, if we are against Communism, we believe that only by education can we convert the Africans into good Portuguese." One is given the image of white and black Portuguese working shoulder to shoulder to build a new Mozambique of towering bridges and dams, busy factories, gleaming schools, and hospitals and churches. It is an image that soon fades.

The Mozambique colony remains sluggish. "This is bad Africa," said a senior official. Tsetse fly still ravages livestock; the climate is sticky and unhealthy; there are few mineral riches. Most investment comes from the Government in the form of strategic roads and airstrips. The South Africans have recently started up a cannery and some hotels, but most foreign business shies away.

"The Mozambique authorities keep saying that the way is open," remarked an English resident, "but nobody comes through." The province depends for its life on the harbor dues of Lourenço Marques and Beira, two of the best ports in Central Africa; on tourism; and, above all, on the money remitted home by hundreds of thousands of blacks working in the mines of South Africa or on the tobacco farms of Southern Rhodesia.

The Portuguese boast of the racially integrated schools, yet more than 90 per cent of the Africans are illiterate. According to official statistics, 370,000 African school pupils, 3,000 teachers and 3,000 schools exist. But quite apart from the fact that only a fraction of the students completes the three-year course in reading and writing, these represent only a tiny proportion of the country's total child population. A liberal said, "There has been a fantastic spurt in education recently which began as a fraud and ended as a good thing." The authorities who, twenty years ago, refused permission to start a boarding school for Africans because it would put ideas into their heads, now truly encourage further education, which is good for Portugal's "image" abroad.

Yet secondary or higher education remains a white privilege. At the Salazar Lycée in Lourenço Marques last year there were 886 white and 17 African children. At the university there are 400 whites and 17 Africans. If one discounts mulattoes the figure is one Negro. Of the total 50 African children in high school at Lourenço Marques last year, 14 were in prison during my stay for having attempted to flee to an independent country.

They had been caught and returned by the Southern Rhodesian police.

Mozambique is not such a smiling land as it at first seems. The PIDE exercise a pervasive and crude supervision and are far more feared than the secret police of South Africa. Indeed, many liberal Portuguese whites have moved to Cape Town and Johannesburg, where they enjoy relative freedom of speech, trial and political action. The police censor every line of every newspaper before publication and often insist that pages be changed several times throughout the night. The mildly radical *Trybuna* has to have its photographs censored as well. One day, for instance, the censors objected to using a photograph of de Gaulle and Sihanouk on the front page. They said it must go to the back page. The next day they objected that it had been tucked away on the back page and wanted it used again, on the front page. Yet, by the standards of metropolitan Portugal, the Mozambique newspapers are considered fairly free. Talking one day with some *Trybuna* journalists, the conversation turned to Tshombe of the Congo, who is beloved by the Portuguese Government but not by Portuguese liberals. I made the (not very funny) description of Tshombe as "the public relations man of destiny." The next day, to my intense surprise, *Trybuna* carried an agency report from Leopoldville under the quite irrelevant headline: "Tshombe: The Public Relations Man of Destiny." Either the censors missed the point or they took the epithet as a compliment. Mozambique, as we shall see, has a special place in its heart for the Public Relations Man.

The white liberals are as strong and eloquent in Mozambique as in metropolitan Portugal. In contrast to South Africa they are found as much among working-class whites as among the intelligentsia. But it is just this intelligentsia of artists, lawyers, journalists, and teachers who set the tone for the opposition—"the poetical opposition" as one left-winger called it. The political dialogue seems more like nineteenth-century Europe than twentieth-century Africa. The white-and-black question enters only marginally into the debate. On the one hand are the establishment of priests, mustached secret policemen and gaudily uniformed army officers. On the other hand, liberals, artists, freemasons, and atheists. It is all rather like Italy under the Habsburgs, and if Puccini's *Tosca* were to be staged in Lourenço Marques a good half of the audience would think of it as a work of social realism.

Much of the white politics is simply Portuguese politics abroad. The more conscientious whites are also worried about the role of Portugal in Africa. They are obliged by the authoritarian régime to confine political agitation to small specific topics such as drainage in the African quarter or the shortage of teachers. Most are privately eloquent about the broader issues. For instance; "Portugal has missed the opportunity of creating a second Brazil here in Africa. After all, the obvious reason why Brazil has been a success is simply that it became independent at the beginning of the last century. The tragedy is that this country might have been a paradise on earth. We have really had very good race relations, and the reforms which the Government is instituting now are really very good ones. But we should have started five hundred years ago instead of in 1961 when trouble broke out in Angola. Now they're bringing a crash program with the result that, for the first time, we have some racial tension. Some of the natives have taken advantage of the increased freedom, while some of the Europeans are beginning to take the example of South Africa and Southern Rhodesia . . . You know, we've done nothing for these people [the Africans] in five hundred years."

The coelocanth, oldest of fish, still lurks in the Gulf of Mozambique. Some wags say that Mozambique is a coelocanth trying to change itself suddenly into a salmon. The Mozambique Portuguese have a fine reputation for political jokes. One joke was of the former Governor of the Province, Admiral Sarmento Rodrigues, who steadfastly refused to mention the name of Salazar in a speech. The wags competed in jokes about Salazar that did not use his name. Another joke was Admiral Rodrigues's successor, General José da Costa Almeida, who was given the job last year with almost no qualification except that of having been born in Mozambique. He was promptly nicknamed "The Unknown Soldier." Some of the jokes are more bitter: "Salazar came home one evening, looking very stiff as usual, in a starched shirt. The young maidservant came in and suggested to the Doctor that he might be more comfortable if he took off his collar. Dr. Salazar agreed. Then the maid suggested he might feel more comfortable if he took off his shirt . . . and then his shoes . . . and then she suggested that she might feel more comfortable if she took off some clothes as well, until they were almost naked. Then the maid suggested they do something naughty. 'Yes, why not?' said Dr. Salazar. 'Hand me that dossier on the African provinces'." The most famous Mozambique joke concerns the statue outside Lourenço Marques Cathedral. It shows a white woman resting her broad, maternal hand on the curly pate of a little African boy. The politically faithful call it Portugal protecting the infant Africa. The jokers say she is measuring him for a job in the mines of Johannesburg. Most jokes are directed against the Portuguese Administration rather than against the liberals or the black Nationalists. Indeed, even supporters of the Government will repeat them.

David Livingstone, who disapproved of the Portuguese in Africa, admitted that no Europeans had a better relationship with the natives. Far from having taboos about sexual relationships with the Africans, they actually encourage them. Indeed, many Portuguese, such as the consul in Johannesburg I have already quoted, actually exaggerate the mongrelization of the Portuguese. To judge by appearances, the Mozambique Portuguese are less racially mixed than, for instance the Afrikaner. This may be because most children of mixed marriages now move into the African rather than the white community. Mixed marriages, once a feature of Mozambique life, are now very rare. But it seems that the Portuguese, like other Latin peoples, do not share the Anglo-Saxon hate-fear of the blacks. They do not, for instance, share the neurotic distaste for touching a black skin. They simply do not understand the kind of hysteria that provoked the South African Parliament to prevent the clothes of whites and blacks being washed in the same laundry.

Whatever their present propaganda, the Portuguese have not, except briefly in the fifteenth century, ever affected to treat the Africans as their equals. At best, their attitude was paternal and kindly; at worst, they treated the blacks like beasts of the field to be worked and exploited without question. Over the centuries there have been different directives from Lisbon about the advancement of the Negroes. A few governors have tried to introduce liberal reforms. But the mass of Portuguese whites have for five hundred years tried to keep the natives as ignorant and submissive cheap labor. When the Portuguese introduced a legal category of *assimilados*, or civilized, Africans it was found that less than one per cent had sufficient educational background to qualify. As late as ten years ago, illiteracy among Africans was almost 99 per cent, and the tiny minority who got through school found it hard to compete for jobs on a level with Europeans.

There was a strong color bar and a pass system in Mozambique until quite recently. One of the few Africans graduate told me over lunch: "Two years ago I wouldn't have been allowed into this restaurant. It's only since Angola that the color bar has really ended. If I'd come in here before I'd have had to bring out a card to show I was an *assimilado*. I think the Government is really trying hard now in education. There are really quite a lot of Africans getting into the schools. But when I started school I was the only black man in the class. There is still only one black lawyer in Mozambique. The very increase in education brings its problems. The blacks can't get jobs in business very easily, so they go into the Government bureaucracy. And there's nothing more terrible than bureaucracy."

We had chanced to take seats in the restaurant next to a table full of South African tourists. At the sight of a black man coming to eat near them they stared as though transfixed with shock. Their eyebrows were quite literally raised. My African acquaintance was not put out. "Really, those South Africans just don't believe or understand what they're doing. They're just frightened of being different from everybody else. I went on the bus to the airport yesterday with a group of South African musicians—mostly black. It was rather crowded and, being polite, I offered my seat to a South African lady. She said 'Thank you' and then exchanged a look with her huband and said, 'No, thank you.' She was pink up to the ears and all these musicians were screaming with laughter."

Even supporters of the Salazar régime profess a great dislike for the apartheid system. One of my guides said how delighted he was to read that the South African team had been kicked out of the Olympic Games: "They offered to send a mixed team, but the point is whether athletes have equal opportunities to train in their own countries." Like other Portuguese officials, he claims to prefer more moderate white Southern Rhodesian politicians like Sir Roy Welensky to extremists like Smith. In fact, there is little in Mozambique that would strike Smith as dangerously radical. "There's no color bar," said the same African friend, "but how many blacks besides me have you seen in a restaurant or café?" The answer was none. Indeed, I saw only one other during the whole of my stay in Portuguese Africa. The color bar of purse and convention is even more harsh in Lourenço Marques than in Salisbury.

The liberal Portuguese, while opposed to South Africa's racial policies, hold up her Government as a model of modern efficiency. "There everything is dynamic and progressive," said a businessman; "here if you want to get anything done you have to fill in forms and plead and beg. Unless you work for the Government or one of the big monopolies it's almost impossible to get anything done. The Administration here is obsessed with the ideas of order, dignity and security. In the Republic it's quite different. As long as you're white there are no controls whatsoever."

A South African liberal living in Mozambique gave a further comparison between the two countries. I could not decide whose side he was really on. "In Angola, the military authorities were very puzzled to find that their troop-carrying trucks were getting shot up, but the supply trucks weren't. Eventually they discovered that the drivers of the trucks were bringing supplies to the rebels in return for a safe-conduct. This is typical of the Portuguese. An Afrikaner would rather see himself and his family *panga'd* than make a deal like that with the Africans."

Up in the north of Mozambique one sees more of the reality of the province than in Lourenço Marques itself. The whites there are less prone to temper their real views with the fashionable multiracialism of the capital. After seven hours of flying we came to Lumbo, where one gets the ferry over to Mozambique Island, the ancient capital of the colony. As the little boat chugged through the swell and one saw the glittering white silhouette of the island rising out of the sea it was difficult to resist a kind of nostalgic admiration for Portugal's career in Africa. Vasco da Gama reached this island in 1498, and his fellow countrymen fought many wars with the Arab slave traders before establishing permanent rule. It remains a tiny museum of colonialism. The two thousand whites live in the northern half of the island in eighteenth-century Portuguese houses of stone, with a warm, pink wash. Plane trees with white-painted trunks line the narrow, cobbled streets. There are lots of baroque churches and bougainvillaea. The ten thousand Africans, Indians and Ismaili Arabs are squeezed more tightly into the other half of the island.

There is an air of colossal but placid boredom. The cashew-nut merchants and civil servants pass the time at cards or at chatting in one of the two clubs or at strolling around the little square with the statue of Vasco da Gama. The explorer looks very plump in this stone likeness, much to the distress of the locals. Three little boys stood in his shadow and started to strum on imaginary guitars, shouting, "Yeah, yeah, yeah." Two demure girls of about eighteen bicycled round and round the island. I watched a half dozen Negroes carry the great sacks of cashew nuts from boats into the depot. Each one, as he took the weight, gasped and staggered and reeled, with muscles trembling from the strain. "The blacks here are no good," said a Portuguese clerk. "They just don't want to work." A series of posters stuck on public buildings told the same story in picture terms. A good black, shown tilling the soil, had a fine suit and a smiling family. A bad black, who preferred the bottle, wore patched clothes and slept under a tree.

The man sitting next to me on the plane heading north had been reading very slowly, banging my ribs with his elbow every time he turned over a leaf; I saw that he was looking at the lives of the saints in strip-cartoon form. The island of Mozambique itself was once a breeding ground of saints. The explorer St. Francis Xavier put in six months at the hospital there on his way to the Far East in 1541. The less well-known Goncalo de Silveira brought Christianity to the Livingstone country three hundred years before the Scottish missionary. The great Portuguese poet Camoens came to the island and wrote of its heroism in the Lusiads. But the early Evangelism soon gave way to lethargy. By the end of the eighteenth century there were less than two thousand Christians in the colony. The priests had become landowners and slave traders. A number of Goan priests proved even more corrupt than the Portuguese, while all the sects bickered among themselves.

There is a plaque up on one of the streets of Mozambique Island to the notable who "expelled the Jesuits and rebuilt Lisbon after the earthquake." I asked a good-natured priest, Father Lazaro, why they recorded this dubious deed. "It was the Republicans at the beginning of the century," he explained, "but nowadays we all get along very well together on the island, even with the Mohammedans." As a matter of fact, the native islanders remain almost entirely Mohammedan even after four hundred and fifty years of Christian missionary work. The women still paint their faces white during the day according to some ancient rite owing more to juju than to cosmetics. The Catholic population of Mozambique is not more than 210,000 even according to Roman Catholic statistics. The nation that boasts so much of its Christian mission in Africa has been strangely unsuccessful in its conversions. Meanwhile, the Government has got rid of most Protestant missionaries, not so much out of doctrinal jealousies but because they tended to put ideas about politics into the heads of the Africans.

The old Governor's Palace on the island is empty now. Even the local District Government has been moved to Nampula, inland. But the state rooms are kept in all their splendor. The bedclothes are kept clean in the four state suites; the gilt chairs are dusted in the magnificent card room where generations of colonists fought back their boredom with whist. The Portuguese have at last decided to open up the wild northern interior, and a fair road joins the coast to Nampula. The Government has tried to open it up by the traditional method of getting poor whites from Europe to take farms. The immigrants do not take easily to this menacing land with its strange, steep mountains rising suddenly out of the plain like points of rock from the ocean. "It got me very depressed here for the first six months," said a Portuguese from the south, "and even now I don't like it."

We came to a cashew farm where the tenant and family were drinking beer out on the porch. The stocky, red-faced man in blue shirt and blue overalls, had been an Army sergeant for six years. Most Portuguese emigrants, he said, went to Brazil, or Venezuela. This was a second best because jobs were not easy to get. He boasted of having seventy-one goats on his farm, but he did not know exactly how many Africans. About forty more or less, he thought. The price for cashew nuts was fairly steady, he said, but this was not a crop on which people grow rich quick. Compared to Angola, this is bad Africa. The majority of Portuguese artisans who come out to Mozambique dream of getting permits to work in the Republic, where pay is at least twice as good. The Portuguese Government plans to move the Government of Mozambique to Nampula as a sign of its determination to remain in the forbidding north, where the Africans are inclined to rebelliousness. Like so many Portuguese plans it is gallant but several centuries late.

People who complain of the inefficiency of independent, black Africa should attempt the journey between Mozambique and Angola, both, in theory, provinces of metropolitan Portugal. We arrived at Beira about noon. The plane was due to leave for Luanda (Angola) at 4 A.M. the next day. During the previous week in Lourenço Marques, we had arranged to have ready in Beira all the necessary papers: first, a rerouting of our tickets; second, two seat reservations on the plane; third, a visa for the Angola province of Portugal. It soon became clear that none of these was prepared and that the last two were considered impossible. Our tickets had been left at the airport; the Portuguese airlines at Beira denied that their office in Lourenço Marques had confirmed our seats; the PIDE in Beira said that they had heard nothing about our request for visas. After fourteen hours of waiting, cajoling, threatening, pleading, sulking and yelling we got all three things. It was a quick course in the remorseless idiocy of the Portuguese bureaucracy.

To compensate for their flagrant inefficiency, the Portuguese set much store by the pleasing influence of public relations departments. They have their own information departments in each province and they obtain further advice from independent public relations consultants in the United States and Great Britain. The British E. D. O'Brien Organization's representative, Cedric Salter, was in Mozambique during my stay. The Portuguese asked and were given his advice as to which British and other foreign journalists should be given visas to cover the forthcoming visit of the President of Portugal. To his credit Mr. Salter recommended a liberal policy towards journalists; but it still seems to me remarkable that the English representative of a London public relations firm should be called on for political advice by the Portuguese authorities in Mozambique.

The E. D. O'Brien of the organization is a jolly, red-faced Irishman with right-wing views and a special interest in Spain, Portugal, Mozambique, Angola and Congo copper. He is a friend and sometimes counselor to that group of M.P.s and businessmen known as the "Katanga Lobby" because of their agitation in favor of Tshombe's breakaway state. His associate, Mr. Salter, has the same self-deprecating sense of humor and, like Mr. O'Brien, had a distinguished career as a journalist, having covered the Spanish Civil War from the Republican side. He is based in Lisbon, but spends much time in Africa on behalf of the Portuguese Government. It is Mr. Salter's job to advise and even arrange the visits of British journalists and M.P.s to Portuguese Africa and to enable them to see for themselves—preferably seeing the showplaces.

The white P.R.O. in Africa now enjoys almost the same status as the white hunter. Many of them are employed by the black countries for their special skill in winning friendship and aid from the West. No white P.R.O. has a finer or more engaging patter than Mr. Salter: "You should really meet the Governor of Carmona in northern Angola. Marvelous fellow. Absolutely fearless. I went with him once up to the Congolese frontier. There was a young Belgian half-caste doctor standing there, so I waved to him and we started talking. He said he was running a hospital for the wounded terrorists about seven miles away. Would we like to come and look at it? I said I'd like to, but that the Governor of a Portuguese province could hardly go across without a visa or anything. The Governor said oh, couldn't he, and we went across. It was a nice hospital with magnificent X-ray equipment but no films for it. The Governor said, 'I've got lots of film over in Angola. I'll go and fetch it.' So he drove back and returned with about thirty pounds' worth of film. The young doctor was ready to kiss him on all four cheeks and salute him with both hands. Rather splendid of the Governor, don't you think?"

Another favorite Salter story concerns an English left-wing journalist who was being shown round a detainment camp in Angola: "A whole lot of children came to greet us with songs and this journalist says, 'Aha! Put-up job.' So I said, 'Of course it's a put-up job. Do you think they go on singing twenty-four hours a day? They've been told we're coming. But just you look at their fat little bellies and happy faces.' Now don't you think that was typical of the left-wing mentality?" Another favorite Salter story: "I talked to one of the terrorists who had been captured in 1961. I asked this chap, 'What are you fighting for?" and he said, 'Freedom.' I said, 'Freedom for what?' This had him thinking a bit. Then he said, 'Freedom to kill the white man and to have the white woman. Then freedom to go into a bank and sign a check and take out money.' 'But before you take out money you have to put in money,' I told him. To which the African said, 'Ah yes, now. But after liberation . . .' "

On arriving from Mozambique at Luanda (Angola)

Airport we were kindly received by no less than three public relations men. Portuguese, English and Italian. The Portuguese works for the Government information department; the Englishman, Mike Chapman, for an American public-relations firm hired by a consortium of American companies working in Angola; the Italian, Mario Pirelli, works on a retainer for the E. D. O'Brien Organization. Altogether in Portuguese Africa I was given the aid of eight different public relations men at one time or another. One of these guides spoke virtually no English and was therefore not much use as an interpreter. Two of them spoke good English, but simply refused to interpret with people whom I wanted to interview but he did not think suitable. I was offered free air travel through Mozambique. I said I would prefer to pay my own fares, but would be glad of official help to avoid trouble with the local authorities. I was told quite bluntly: "I'm afraid if you don't accept the air fare you won't get official help."

The Portuguese authorities in Africa have long been suspicious of Anglo-Saxon critics of their régime. The recent Angolan uprising and subsequent protest from foreign liberals is nothing new. There were even more bloody native wars in Angola and in Mozambique at the turn of the century. Just as Basil Davidson, the *New Statesman* and the Labor Party have lambasted Portuguese rule in this decade, so Henry Nevinson, the *Spectator* and the Liberal Party lambasted it in the 1900s. Then, as now, the Portuguese replied with hurt reminders that they were our oldest ally. Then, as now, they denounced all criticism as inspired by the nonconformist sects and Anglo-American imperialism. The only difference is that they now try to fend off criticism by the use of public relations consultants.

Then, as now, the Portuguese have tried to compensate for the failure of their native policy by importing immigrants from the mother country. Since 1961, when fighting broke out in Luanda and the North, nearly a hundred thousand more Portuguese have come into the province, of whom at least forty thousand are troops. Some of these have been given farms in the settlement areas, but thousands have gone to live in the African slums of Luanda and other big cities, where they live as neighbors with the Africans. In one such district of Luanda, I talked with newly arrived immigrants working as tailors, cobblers or merchants of tinned goods, oil, soap and glasses of red biddy.

Since Portugal has by far the lowest standard of living in Europe it is hardly surprising that these immigrants should tolerate squalor. Building a house takes two weeks. As they explained, "You just go down to the Casa Americana where they import automobiles and you buy yourself the packing case from a Cadillac or a Chev and there you have yourself a house." Sometimes the frame is made from criss-cross slats of wood with bits of metal or broken drain pipe threaded between. The whole thing is covered with mud from the street outside, and this takes about three days to dry. All these mud-hut dwellers, white and black, assured me that the houses kept well even during the rainy season. Sometimes these poor whites do up the inside with pride. Four sisters, all seamstresses from Lisbon, had decorated their hovel with a portrait of the President of Portugal, a group photograph of the Ben Fica Football Club and an enormous advertisement for Fresh Up, showing a group of elegant young getting out of a car in Chelsea or Manhattan. A poster outside their door says, "Angola, ever bigger, ever better, even more Portuguese." After six years in Luanda they had saved up enough to buy an electric sewing machine.

"If you've got a Portuguese anywhere," one man said, "you won't find a Jew anywhere in the neighborhood. They work hard, strike a hard bargain and don't mind sleeping under the counter at night." In spite of the race riots in 1961, they do not fear living among the poor Africans. These Portuguese shopkeepers dream of saving enough to go into real business. In northern Angola, in terrorist country, I met one such man who had made good.

José Cagida, aged sixty-one, has six thousand hectares of coffee plantation spread over several farms. He employs twelve whites and four hundred blacks, and his machinery for shelling and drying the coffee beans is modern even by Kenya standards. He has a sallow face, a drooping Mexican-bandit moustache, dark rims round the eyes and a gold-toothed, open-mouthed laugh. Stalking about his estate in his ten-gallon hat with an Italian shotgun over his shoulder, he described how he had made good. "My story is complicated. I was a young boy of seventeen when I came to Africa. At this time there was no railway and no road. I had to come up from the coast by foot. My uncle had given me the money to come to Africa, and I was helping to run a shop on the coast. But I had only five escudos to my name, although, mind you, in those days five escudos would buy you a pair of shoes. When I came up here two friends were starting a company and they asked me to help. I was very lucky—I am a very lucky man. In the year I started the price of coffee went up from 15 to 115 escudos and in that year I earned 300 contos . . . When I came here the grass was five metres high. I killed elephants where you are standing now. When I wanted meat there was six thousand kilos of it . . . During the troubles nothing happened on this estate, thank God. I am a very lucky man." He is almost reverent about his estate. One hillside with towering, ghostly gum trees he calls "my cathedral." At another view he remarked, "Here one can speak with the gods." His wife and family live in Portugal, as do most families from the trouble area.

Like many middle-aged men temporarily separated from their wives and family, Mr. Cagida and his set comfort themselves at the table. "Yesterday we had a Portuguese meal," he explained, "codfish and boiled potatoes. Tomorrow you will have an African meal: bean soup, sardines with tomatoes; then chicken with hot pepper. Also pigeons and good wine with it." Both meals were indeed excellent. One day he complained of having eaten too much for breakfast. "Yes," said his Goan friend, "he ate two dishes of fish." At which Mr. Cagida gave one of

SOUTH AFRICA: Crowd at a Johannesburg rugby game

ANGOLA: Portuguese girl in the slums of Luanda

IVORY COAST: An African now living in the former "white district" of town

ZAMBIA: White girls from South African or Southern Rhodesian mining families

TH AFRICA: Johannesburg football fan

NIGER: A bar in Niamey. In blazing subsaharan heat Frenchmen down ice-cold drinks while gazing at a huge photograph
of alpine snows.

SOUTH AFRICA: A white beggar woman in a Johannesburg street

IVORY COAST: Two leading French businessmen of Abidjan

ZAMBIA: A young South African miner

KENYA: White farmers at a wedding party in the "White Highlands"

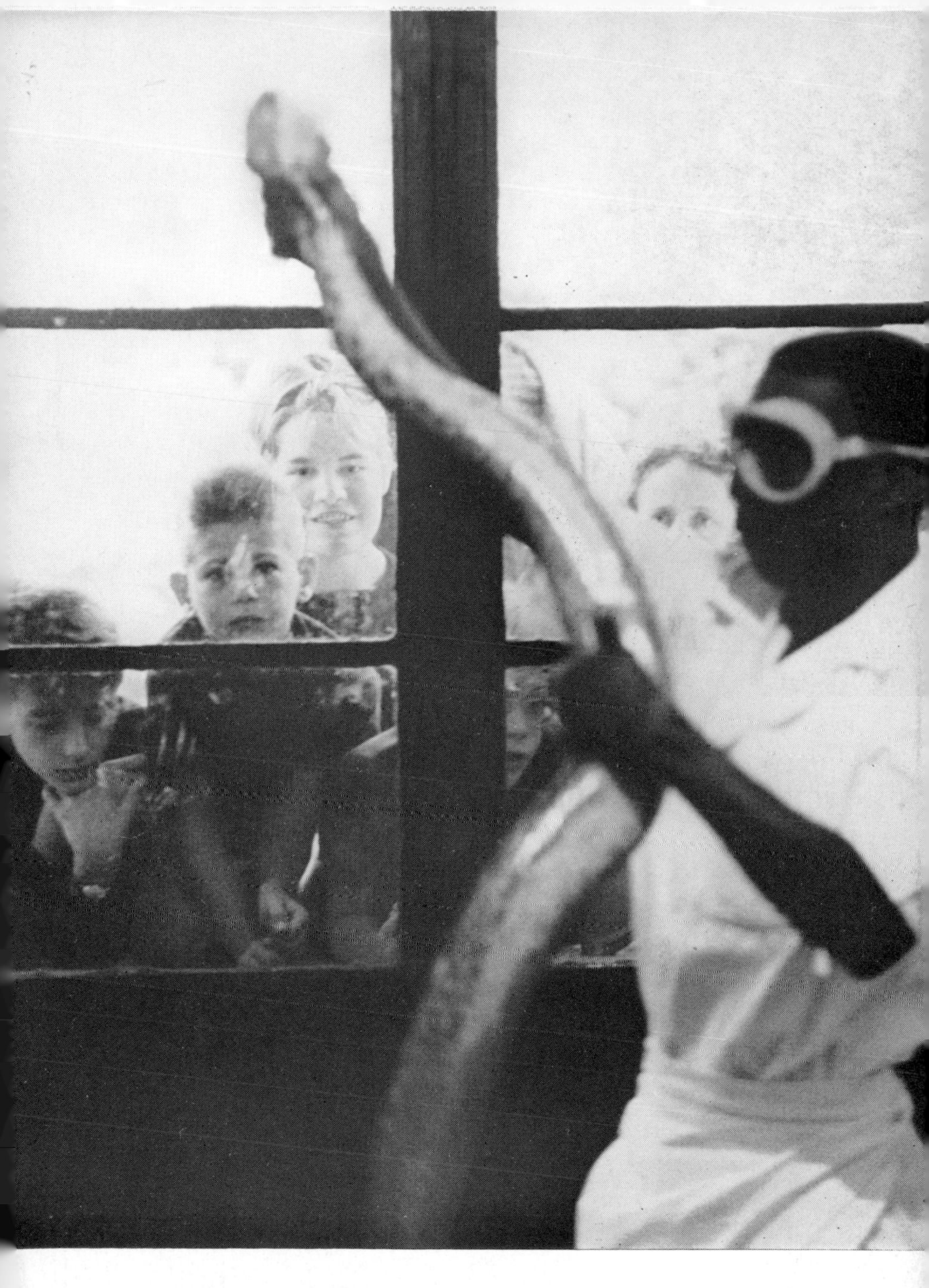

CONGO REPUBLIC (formerly the French Congo): Watching poison being taken from a Gaboon viper at the Pasteur Institue in Brazzaville

SOUTH AFRICA: Afrikaner (Boer) farmer in the Rand

CONGO: Belgian nun and priest with Africans in Leopoldville

ANGOLA: White Portuguese living alongside Africans in the Luanda slums

SOUTH AFRICA: Poor whites in Johannesburg

CONGO: Robert Cohen of Elisabethville, a boxing trainer

KENYA: Wedding guests in the "White Highlands"

his Mexican-bandit laughs. Another day he arrived with antelope meat, wrapped in vine leaves. Again the Mexican-bandit laugh. Then he talked about a departed friend, a Goan, and sighed. He had been such a marvelous cook for Indian specialities. He cheered himself with a drink from the favorite glass which his wife had given him. Made in England, it is decorated with pictures of two grinning blacks carrying a white woman struggling to the cooking pot. It was curious to see this glass cause such amusement in a district where several hundred white women had in fact been killed, although not, in all probability, eaten.

Like most of the coffee planters we met, Mr. Cagida is cool in his attitude to the Africans. The Bakongo people, who are indigenous to this Portuguese Congo district, are feared and disliked by the whites. Always the most mutinous of the tribes, they led the uprising in 1961 and were in turn savagely massacred by the whites in what is euphemistically called "the reaction to the events." At least a quarter of a million Bakongo people are still living as refugees in the Congo Republic, among their fellow tribesmen. Practically none now work on the plantations. "They lack confidence," said one farmer, meaning they fear the whites. The whites also fear the Bakongo. "If you want a servant," said another white, "don't take one of these people. You'll get robbed. They are the worst people in the Congo." The Portuguese much prefer the tribes from the south, who are more docile, more backward and less ambitious.

Most of the black troops in the Portuguese Army

come from southern Angola. The total forces in northern Angola number about 40,000, matched against 2,000–5,000 rebels hidden up in the dank rain forests towards the Congolese border. At the barracks of the 3rd Battallion Chasseurs in Carmona, both white and black soldiers were weeding the floral badge of the regiment on the law. Their Colonel Diego, a dyspeptic man with a pained Humphrey Bogart face, stressed the multiracialism of Portugal's forces: "When they go off to fight, sometimes all one company is black. Often you have black sergeants leading white troops. They eat the same food, sleep in the same barracks and get the same pay. Often the blacks cry when they have to leave the Army." These regular Army troops are mostly conscripts; many of them are armed with turn-of-the-century Mausers. It is a grueling, hot campaign chasing the rebels, but casualties are low. The rebels avoid combat with the troops, preferring to slip across the Congolese frontier when things get difficult.

Life is probably worse for the civilian whites than for the Army. The rebels often attack outlying coffee plantations and unprotected motorcars. While we were there they ambushed a pair of cars, killed four men and left one barely alive with fourteen bullets inside him. Our civilian guide told us several times how he had himself been decorated for "bravery and gallantry although I have not taken part in any fighting." The guerilla war does not arouse the same passion as Mau Mau did. Although terrible atrocities were committed by both sides in 1961, there have been no obscene rites or oath-taking, no ritual torture of prisoners.

The hatred of the Portuguese civilians is directed not so much at the black rebels as at the whites who they think give them aid. A Carmona journalist, newly arrived from Lisbon, roared out his defiance with all the belligerence of a civilian: "The Americans have betrayed us. The English, our oldest allies, are against us. The Belgians are all pederasts and the Vatican is our enemy. But even if metropolitan Portugal deserts us, we shall stay firm. We shall never forget that the terrorists chopped up our friends. If Salazar is a Fascist, then I am a Fascist. What is my definition of Fascism? It is love of my country, love of my family and love of God." As he said this, rolls of fat rippled up and down his neck in indignation.

The old-timers were not quite so belligerent, not quite so sure. Some wondered about the Church's attitude. "Jesus Christ was a liberal," one of them said in a mixture of indignation and puzzlement. They started to argue about the history of Portugal in Africa. What year had it been that Mousinho de Albuquerque had won his triumphs in Mozambique? They settled the dispute not by reference to an encyclopedia but to the *Jornal do Exercito*, a magazine of military affairs told in strip-cartoon form.

Congo

THE VERY NAME "Congo" strikes terror in most African whites. It had been so for at least a century before the troubles of independence in 1960. This immense tract of jungle and forest, covering almost the same space as India, was the scene of Joseph Conrad's novel, *Heart of Darkness.* To the imagination it has always been a place of cannibalism, slavery, crocodiles, gorillas, driver ants and the black mamba snake, which has been known to chase and kill a galloping horse and rider. It is the classic country of raped nuns and stewed missionaries, of Pygmies and poisoned blowdarts, of voodoo and leprosy. King Leopold II of the Belgians developed the Congo until early this century when it was handed over to the state. The cruelty of the régime was legendary. African workers for the ivory and rubber traders were punished for laziness by the amputation of a hand. It is reliably said that Leopold's rule cost over five million lives in a country of twenty million. The population now is about fifteen million. The atrocities of the Congo today, although frightful, are probably slightly less bad than those of the Leopold régime. The difference is that in 1900 they were committed by white people against the blacks, and they were not shown on television.

Since 1960 the white African attitude to the Congo has been further colored by political partisanship. The European-controlled newspapers in East Africa, Southern Rhodesia, South Africa and the Portuguese territories print more about the Congo than almost the rest of Africa put together. Sometimes this is justified by important news. Often it is merely a means of suggesting that Africans are incapable of self-government. Almost any speech by a right-wing politician in Lourenço Marques or Johannesburg is likely to have a reference to the horrors of the Congo. One of Ian Smith's colleagues in Southern Rhodesia recently used the Congo to illustrate his attacks on the press, which he thinks dangerously left-wing. "Why don't they go to the Congo and see for themselves?" he asked the crowd, pointing an angry accusing finger towards the press table. The speaker himself had not been to the Congo. All four journalists had; indeed, one of those present was shot and badly wounded in Katanga.

Even liberal whites tell ghoulish stories about the Congo. Before going there, I had been warned that cannibalism was on the increase; that white fingers were considered a special delicacy; that there were no hotel rooms available in the Congo; that all the shops had been closed; that piles of rubbish stood waist high in the city streets; that white people were frequently beaten up in full view of the police; that any white car driver thought guilty of a traffic offense was obliged by the police to practice changing gears for as long as six hours in front of the police station; that Congo malaria was so powerful that all prophylactics were useless; that all the main roads were infested with brigands.

This last charge has some substance, and it was not in a cheerful mood that John Bulmer and I set off in a hired car from Ndola, in Northern Rhodesia, to Elisabethville. This was shortly before the U.N. moved out of Katanga, and we were hoping to join one of the car convoys run by the Ethiopian U.N. troops. The Northern Rhodesian frontier post asked us to report with them at 3:30 in order to join the convoy. We arrived there to find that no convoy was leaving that day, but they said that other cars had gone through, so we were slightly encouraged to go on alone. We drove across to the Congolese customs immigration post, where an official, in saucer-sized dark glasses, requested us to accept two fellow travelers. One was the center forward of the Nchanga Rangers—"they call me the spoiler"—the other a sullen young soldier, also in dark glasses. As we set off he pushed three bullets into his rifle breech and sat back with the muzzle pointing at his head. The drive to Elisabethville was uneventful, but not without anxiety. The Congo roads are rather like the wagon trails of the old Wild West. It is Indian country. And you may not know until too late whether the Indians are friendly. The numerous gangs of bandits have a single method of work. They get uniforms and guns and then stop the first passing car to rob and generally kill its occupants. The legitimate soldiers and *gendarmerie* also operate constant road checks, and it is quite impossible to guess beforehand which are bandits dressed as soldiers and which are soldiers dressed as bandits. A great many motorists, most of them Europeans, have been murdered in Katanga. On the other hand, thanks to the lack of traffic, the actual number of deaths on the road is lower in the Congo than in Great Britain.

The road to Elisabethville is lined with many wrecked and burned-out automobiles. In the southern suburbs I saw the sign "Les Amis du Congo" over a gutted shop. This was the scene of some fighting and much looting during hostilities between the United Nations and Mr. Moise Tshombe's breakaway Katanga republic. A colossal copper spoil heap dominates the south side of town, gleaming in dark rich colors like a beetle's back. The center of town is rather desolate. Most of the shops are boarded up; the streets, many still named after Belgian kings and queens, are frequently blocked by road checks, checking goodness knows what. But the Leopold II Hotel offers clean rooms and very good food. There are many excellent restaurants and night clubs. "This is heaven compared to Leopoldville," says an American civil pilot. "That's really Endsville. There ain't a nigger there's done a stroke of work in four years." He comes from a Southern state and claims that, after a recent low-flying mission in Kivu province, he found two arrows stuck in the fuselage of his plane.

Of course, the Belgians are still, overwhelmingly, the

most numerous of the Europeans in the Congo. They have had a bad press throughout the world, and one U.N. official—not an impartial witness—called them the Congolese of Europe. Foreigners, and particularly the English, take a holier-than-thou attitude to the Belgians and suggest, sometimes publicly, that if *they* had been running the Congo the transition to independence would have gone much more smoothly. This seems to me rather unfair. Belgian colonial policy may have been very misguided; there was no attempt to train a professional class of Africans and no plan for the transference of power until the last-minute scuttle. But from all accounts there was nothing wicked about the Belgians working in the Congo. They were not allowed to own land except for parts of the northeastern cattle country. They were not encouraged to stay in the Congo more than a few years and they were not allowed to come at all without putting up a substantial bond to the Government. If the blacks had no vote, no more did the fifty thousand Belgians. There were no poor whites as in Rhodesia and no white-settler political groups as in Kenya. "Perhaps they did flash their wealth around," said an English old Congo hand, "especially the women loaded with jewels in the hotels by Lake Kivu, but they were tolerant with the Africans. There was less color bar here than in the British colonies." There are no more tourists—only terrorists—by Lake Kivu; and I saw no Belgian women with jewelry. But the Belgians are back in the Congo in almost as great numbers as before.

There are thirteen thousand Europeans in Elisabethville alone. At least sixty civilians have been killed since independence. The rest have become almost indifferent to violence. "Frankly we get blasé about shooting here," said a stalwart of the golf clubs. "If there's shooting as much as half a mile away we don't take any notice. But golf stops if there's mortar fire." The British are not the only ones with stiff upper lips. An Elisabethville housewife described to me how once she had joined her friends for the start of lunch when firing broke out at the other end of town. She dashed home, of course, but "not before gulping down a few oysters and some of the wine. They were still flying oysters in at that time." The city has long been under threat of invasion; by Baluba tribesmen, by the United Nations, by the Congolese National Army or by the Chinese-trained forces of Mr. Sumialot. Many Belgians learn the latest threat each morning at the little café across the road from the Leopold II. It is the natural center of rumor and truth, a kind of animated newspaper. There is always something fresh to worry about. When I was there the authorities had impounded all Belgian passports.

The atmosphere of violence goes with a pervasive dullness. A Belgian, out there for twelve years, complained, "There used to be a Flemish Club and a Walloon Club, but people now don't go out in the evening. They stay at home or play cards with the neighbors. It's not that they're frightened of bandits, but there are many burglars about. One man the other day went out to the cinema and came back to find his house stripped." They keep saying how Elisabethville used to be a Belgian town. Now it is plainly African. There are no cozy billiard saloons, no cafés with beer and buttered potatoes. It has often occurred to me abroad that you can learn a lot about a society by studying the pictures on show in a photographer's shop. The one in Elisabethville caters to both whites and blacks, of course. The African photographs almost all showed either two women hand in hand or a soldier in blotch-camouflage uniform holding a vase. Both these favorite poses seem perfectly suited to the Congolese. The Belgians' favorite photographs were of pubescent girls in first-communion dresses, either at prayer, of rolling their eyes skyward. This is the homely, suburban picture to comfort the Belgian exiled in the Congo. It is not the sort of photograph one would have found in the knapsack of a Stanley or a Livingstone.

The boredom is often expressed in aggressiveness, and Elisabethville is the holy city of all saloon-bar brawlers. The American pilot quoted earlier appeared one day with a black eye after announcing in a bar that the Belgians did not really belong in the Congo. Two of the five men who had beaten him up tried in a desultory way to quarrel with me, by muttering insults. On the other side two very lugubrious Belgians were telling me about the good old days: "It was the people who came out here after the second war who spoiled everything. They started talking politics and giving ideas to the Africans. Before the war nobody ever talked of politics." His companion, who had "lost millions" from independence, kept interjecting the ever more slurred refrain, "Bring back forced labor."

Most of the wealth of Katanga comes from the Union Minière, the giant copper company which backed the breakaway Katangese republic. Considering that it is probably the most controversial company in the world, the Union Minière is shy of publicity and cameras. "It is not the policy of the company for directors to be photographed," said an official in Elisabethville. "Have you ever seen a photograph of a Union Minière executive? No? Well, you see!" The mines stretch along the Rhodesian border as far as Jadotville. It is a world of stern industrial order within the political anarchy of the Congo. Most of the black miners come from Ruanda-Burundi, and the foremen come from Belgium. They have good homes here and good money, which they can save. Their wives and children are happy, too, but they complained of a lack of security.

Economic life is not so good for some of the smaller businessmen. The traders have been hit by the import regulations and exchange controls. A general wholesaler pointed out an advertisement for Bint El Sudan scent: "It's a perfume for Africans. Very strong. But we can't buy it any more. Much of what we sell now is Congolese-made and it costs three times as much as what we imported." This wholesaler, Robert Cohen, is better known as the former bantam-weight champion of the world, and he now runs a gymnasium for Congolese boxing amateurs. "I put an advertisement in the papers six years ago asking if any African wanted to learn to box. I do it free, you know. We did have one European training, but the Europeans don't like to train with Africans." Mr. Cohen said that he had come to the Congo "for love. I got married. That's why I left boxing, too."

There used to be a big colony of Sephardic Jews in Elisabethville, but most seem to have gone. The 3,500 Greeks control most of the small shops in Eastern Congo. There are a thousand in Elisabethville alone, and their excellent restaurants are complete with *kebabs*, *retsina* and *bazouki* music. Unhappily, the import restrictions have cut down the supply of olive oil. Many of these Greeks are second-generation Africans and have never been back home. The Reverend Father Emmanuel Zoppas, Vicar to the Orthodox Archbishop of Central Africa at Evangelismos Cathedral, has not been home to Rhodes for nearly thirty years. "We suffered badly during the *événements*. In some areas all the Greek shops were robbed and burned. Most of the Greek population went away during the *événements*, but now they'll all come back." The cathedral, built in 1958, is profusely hung with chandeliers and icons from Greece. "I made a journey of three and a half months through the Congo," the Vicar told me, "collecting money from all the Greeks. All the decorations were gifts from families. I went to all the families and said, for instance, 'You give me an icon of the Virgin' or 'You give a St. Nicholas.' They gave a million and a half francs."

The Greek Orthodox Church does not bother to try to convert the Africans. It is one of the few in that respect. An English Evangelical, A. E. Nock, is one of many veteran missionaries in the Congo. He has been there thirty-six years, including the troubles when his house in the north was sacked and his next house in Elisabethville was stormed by Baluba rebels armed with knives and hatchets. How many Congolese were Christians, I asked. "It would seem that about three million come under the heading of Christian. But we don't necessarily classify them as Christian unless they deliver the goods. The Catholics classify them as Christians if they put a cloth round their middles. The Protestants are much more reserved. We ourselves [Evangelicals] think we have fifteen thousand in communion." He seemed dispirited about the future: "When there's anything to be done in his country, whether religious or secular, the summits are always held by Europeans, whether it's doctors who can train or expositors of the Gospel . . . This country becomes less and less interesting, far more difficult to live in . . . The Europeans here are mixing water with their wine. The African is coming back to his senses, but for two or three years there was quite a lot of feeling against the whites. Not so much against the missionaries, but a lot against the traders, especially the Greeks. And not without reason. I don't know what they're like in Europe, but here most of them are just out for their bank balance. During the troubles, when the Europeans tended to gather together for protection, to get water and food, for instance, the Greeks wouldn't do anything to help."

There was something dour and depressing about all

the Evangelical missionaries I met in the Congo. By contrast, it was a great joy to visit a school run by Roman Catholic nuns in the bush about eight miles east of Elisabethville. They were members of the Salesian order and almost all Flemish, although they could speak French. The mother superior told us that five of the nuns and most of the African pupils were holding a picnic out in the bush a few miles away to celebrate the end of examinations the day before. Would we care to join them there? It turned out to be a camping site used also by schoolboys; there was a broken sign in one clearing inscribed "Croco Patrol." And scouting, for once, coincided with life, for there were indeed crocodiles in the stream below the picnic place. One of the beasts had recently eaten a child a few miles downstream. A nun, Sister Eliza, must have noticed my distaste for deadly animals. "Don't worry," she said, "this isn't the bad season for snakes. But recently they found a python near here coiled round a dog. They ran for one of the *frères*, who brought his gun and shot it in the head. They haven't got its mate yet. You know, the mate always comes back. They shot it in the back, but didn't kill it." Sister Eliza was no more frightened of brigands than of wild beasts: "They had to shut a school nearby because of banditry, but we've not had much trouble here. The only trouble came from some of the local people. Some young men *noviciens* came out from Belgium, and because they were young and European the Africans thought they must be from the U.N."

There were some sixty girls on the picnic, all boarders

and mostly from simple families in the bush. They were clearly good at the practical business of camping. They had brought the pots and pans on their heads, collected firewood, and split up into teams to do the cooking of the food, which they baked in mud. "They're marvelous at camping," said Sister Thérèse, a young, pretty nun in dark glasses, who reminded me of a girl in London. "They're far more practical than we are. As soon as they get here they split into teams of ten. They take responsibility very easily. No quarreling at all. There's a marvelous spirit among them." Both nuns and girls were in happy end-of-term mood. They sang songs, experimented with some of the girls' hair styles, and screamed with laughter. "*Sérieusement, un, deux, trois . . .*" chanted Sister Eliza in an effort to stop giggling, then gave it up, playfully knocked one of the girl's turbans off and led an expedition down to the riverside.

These five nuns, one of them Congolese, obviously loved the children and their job. "They're really sweet," said Sister Thérèse, "no trouble at all. They are naturally disciplined, and all you have to do is treat them gently. They love their studies; they have a passion for learning." At the same time these children had an uninhibited gaiety, curiosity and high spirit of the kind that is sought but so seldom found in progressive schools in Europe. At the end of the day the nuns and the children loaded the camping equipment onto their heads and set off in file to walk home through the Congo forest. They sang "Swing Low, Sweet Chariot" in faulty English, and the whole column waved to us as we drove off. That tune, the friendly smiles of the nuns and the big orange-peel grins of their African pupils have remained clear in my memory as the most moving moment experienced in Africa. I am neither a religious believer nor sentimental about children. It was not the piety of the nuns that impressed us but their goodness and, above all, happiness in the cruel and tragic Congo.

It is good to think of those nuns when one hears the stories, told often by people who have not been there, of Belgian cowardice in the Congo. They are accused of bolting across the border whenever rebels attack; of spreading alarmist atrocity stories; in short, of letting the white side down. It is true that in parts of Kivu and Kwilu provinces the isolated Belgians have often escaped from the civil war. I do not blame them. Rumors always fester in a country where order has collapsed. But if the Belgians were really cowardly, they would not consent to stay in the Congo. Some ten thousand Europeans, mostly Belgians, teach in schools all over this huge country. Although the pay is good, they surely would not accept the work unless they felt some commitment to Africa. I met several of these men and women on their way back to Europe for summer holidays, after a year of teaching in the discomfort and loneliness of the jungle. One man, a Belgian who keeps in touch with the world through the English magazines, was desperate for information. "What do they think in London? Is Iain Maclayodd a good editor of the *Spectator?* Tell me, please, What is this new book by Evelyn Wog?" Certainly many Belgians feel afraid in the Congo. So do most people. There is plenty to be afraid of. Ten times as many Belgians have been killed in the Congo since 1960 than British were killed in Kenya during the Emergency.

On the plane from Elisabethville to Leopoldville, I met Godefroide Munongo, old henchman of Moise Tshombe, and now Minister of the Interior. A huge, dark-spectacled man, with the broad smile of a shark, he is reputed to have been the killer of Lumumba. To many Europeans, and especially the journalists, he is the representative politician for this heart of darkness. On this plane ride Mr. Munongo talked for a bit in the first-class section, then moved to address the predominantly Belgian passengers in the back: "When we enter the Congo," he said, for in his eyes Katanga was still a separate state, "you will see who is boss. It is *le patron* [Mr. Tshombe]." The passengers smiled a little nervously.

Leopoldville was in its habitual state of crisis. Politicians were coming back from exile. A bomb had exploded among a queue of voters outside a polling station. Another had wounded some wedding guests at the zoo, which is also a favorite place for political meetings. There was a curfew at nights, and several night clubs had retaliated by opening house at ten o'clock in the morning. Traffic was closed with Brazzaville across the river, the capital of the other, former French Congo. This was about the time of the fourth anniversary of independence, and a bitter joke was going the rounds, concerning the big capitaine fish which are a delicacy in the Congo. In honor of independence, so the story goes, all the capitaines were about to be promoted to colonel. The United Nations troops were leaving as well, to the great glee of the Belgians. Some Belgians summed up for me their impressions of the United Nations troops in the Congo: "The best were the Malayans. Very polite. Very calm. Then the Gurkhas, then the Ethiopians. Worst of all were the Swedes, and I'm afraid the Irish weren't much better." Of course, they may have been prejudiced. Dag Hammarskjöld was a Swede, and Conor Cruise O'Brien, another Belgian bogy figure, is an Irishman.

The first night in Leopoldville was sleepless. The air conditioner did not work, nor could it be switched off. It kept up a continuous asthmatic growl, broken at ten-minute intervals by a crash as loud as a *plastique*. Mosquitoes swarmed through the broken netting, aiming with bloodthirsty persistence at the inside of the nostrils. The city, so they say, was not always like this. "Leopoldville is sprayed by helicopters carrying D.D.T. every night," wrote John Gunther, who visited there in the early fifties. Such a thing would be unimaginable today. But economic life goes on in the great stained and sweating office blocks.

A curious feature of the Belgians: most of those in the Congo are Flemish, yet they almost always speak French, even among themselves. An Englishman who had traveled out on a Belgian boat said that all the passengers spoke Flemish until putting down in the Congo, when they immediately broke into French. The Africans invariably refer to Belgians as "*les Flamands*," and the term is not always flattering. Another Englishman described going to the "gents" at an African dance hall and finding himself standing next to a Congolese. The Congolese turned and said simply, "*Sale Flamand!*" The Englishman, looking as dignified as possible in such a place, answered, "Dirty I may be, but Flemish not." He and the Congolese then had a drink together.

The Belgians like to believe that the Congolese regret the days of colonialism. "When my servant heard I was going to Elisabethville," said a Leopoldville housewife, "he said, 'Please, buy me some shirts and trousers. There they still have the Flemish prices. Here we have the independence prices.' " Independence has certainly soured the feelings of many Belgians towards the Congolese. Under colonialism there was a fairly respectful although paternalist relationship. But a Belgian who was persistently rude to Africans could be shipped home to Europe; anyone calling an African "monkey" was fined £7. An Elisabethville shopkeeper described to me how she had lost her temper with the police for their callous indifference to a man badly wounded in a traffic accident, and had worked off her feelings afterwards by calling the Congolese monkeys. There was no fine, but her staff had threatened to strike in protest. The Congolese were and are particularly sensitive to this term of abuse from whites. On one occasion we saw some of them hanging from branches of trees to look over the wall into a football match. They protested vehemently against being photographed: "We are men!"

Many Europeans become rather strange in the Congo.

It was noticeable even among the journalists who had been sent there to cover the troubles. After a time they tended to twitch, to disappear for days on end, to wander about their hotel rooms in pitch darkness, or to think they could solve the Congo's political problems. Much of the day is spent over the telex machines in the Leopoldville Central Post Office, which is used by the *gendarmerie* as a latrine. The rest of the day is spent sifting the contradictory rumors of murder, battle and treachery from all parts of the great republic. Some of these journalists comfort themselves with rereading Conrad's *Heart of Darkness.* "Ten minutes of it before breakfast and I can face the day," said a colleague on one of the London dailies. It is still the definitive work on what it feels like to be in the Congo.

The narrator of this story is a captain who had been sent to run a steamer on a mighty big river "that you could see on the map, resembling an immense snake uncoiled, with its head in the sea, its body at rest curving afar over a vast country, and its tail lost in the depths of the land." As they move up this river the Congo horrors unfold: the shackled criminals, the flogging, the impaled heads, the stench of rotting hippo meat, and the appalling Congo weather. "When the sun rose there was a white fog, very warm and clammy, and more blinding than the night. It did not shift or drive; it was just there, standing all around you, like something solid. At eight or nine, perhaps, it lifted as a shutter lifts. We had a glimpse of the towering multitude of trees, of the immense matted jungle, with the blazing little ball of the sun hanging over it—all perfectly still—and then the white shutter came down again, smoothly, as if sliding in greased grooves." The narrator goes in search of a Mr. Kurtz, ivory hunter, perhaps a journalist, who is writing a report for the International Society for the Suppression of Savage Customs. The report begins with elevated sentiments—"by the simple exercise of our will we can exert a power for good practically unbounded"—and ends with a phrase, added much later in an unsteady hand, "Exterminate all the brutes!" The narrator meets the dying Kurtz and brings back his letters to his fiancée in London. The girl asks the narrator what had been Kurtz's last words, and he lyingly says, "The last word he pronounced was—your name." In fact, Kurtz's last words had been, "The horror! The horror!" The narrator says of his voyage down the coast to the Congo, "Nowhere did we stop long enough to get a particularized impression, but the general sense of vague and oppressive wonder grew upon me. It was like a weary pilgrimage amongst hints for a nightmare."

Even in the Congo many white people comfort themselves with the idea that things are worse in the next country. They are worried about the influence of Communism and of the Chinese in particular—in Tanganyika. As if the Congo itself were not mutilated enough by rumor, the Europeans have to discuss the latest rumors in Dar es Salaam. Here, as in many African countries, people whisper about the document that proves one of the Tanganyikan leaders a Communist. I have, in fact, seen this odd intelligence report of which so much is rumored. It proves no more than that the Minister had once visited Israel and that he wanted to Africanize the Tanganyikan Army. This pathetically dull document was used in evidence, in the Congo, of a Communist plot to seize the continent. In Africa it is always the next country which is cracking up.

"Bingo, Bango, Bongo, I don't wanna leave the Congo, oh, no, no, no, no . . ." The words and tune of the once popular song kept coming back with flesh-creeping irony. One wanted desperately to leave the Congo. One evening I had a dreadful nightmare, about London, and woke sweating and gasping with that thankful joy at being back in the real world. A dog or a jackal howled. It was three o'clock in the morning in Elisabethville, and the real world seemed little better. Most Europeans hate the Congo, but . . . it remains the one African country to which they long to return. I cannot even write about it without a surge of nostalgia. Even Conrad's hymn of hate has an undertone of admiration. There is something about that immense jungle anarchy that inspires awe. Even the terror is partly pleasurable. The narrator of *Heart of Darkness* was obliged to see a doctor before making the voyage to Africa: " 'I always ask leave, in the interests of science, to measure the crania of those going out there,' he said. 'And when they come back, too?' I asked. 'Oh, I never see them,' he remarked, 'and, moreover, the changes take place inside, you know . . .' "

Former French Africa and Gambia

AFTER THE Portuguese Congo and former Belgian Congo it was pleasant, at first, to be in the former French Congo, or Congo-Brazzaville. When I strolled out in the morning two little boys approached with outstretched hands and I turned aside with the usual sour look of people avoiding beggars. But they merely wished to shake hands and say, "Bon joo, M'ieu, bon joo." Both men and women here dress in loud yellow and blue cotton which goes with their constant, loud, unspoken jokes against you, the visitor. There are less than a million people in Congo-Brazzaville, and the soil produces little but manioc, bananas and avocado pears—of which there is no shortage in Africa. Yet except for a revolution last year which scarcely made the British newspapers, this tiny bit of Congo is calm. Immediately one begins to think that they manage things better in former France.

But when the civilization of France confronts the Congo it is the Congo that wins. We drove down to a beat café beside the swamp formed by one of the tributaries of the Congo. The café was closed, but we met a Frenchman carrying a small cayman in a cage. He was taking it back to the Pasteur Institute, where he worked. With him was an African girl of about eight or nine, with her hair done up in stalks from her pate. "We call her Sputnik," he said, "and she's a clever girl, but they haven't got the money to send her to school." Sputnik and the Frenchman had not only the cayman but a big iguana lizard in a cage the size of a hen coop. The creature clung to the wire at the side with a dazed frightened look, as well it might, for its tail would soon be cut off and boiled for the *plat du jour* of an African dinner. I prepared to leave and reached to shake hands with the Frenchman. He muttered some excuse and offered me his left hand. I looked again and saw that his right hand and arm were made of dark brown plastic.

He was perfectly willing to explain. Apparently he was a reptile specialist at the Pasteur Institute and it had been his job to help extract the venom each month from the collection of Gabon vipers. One day the African assistant dropped the snake "which struck at my right arm. The whole arm began to turn black, and then the whole right side of my body. This happened right in the Institute with serum handy, but I had taken such a huge quantity of poison that the situation was very serious. First they cut off my hand, and I thought all right, then my arm up to the elbow and then up to the shoulder. I thought to myself I can do without an arm, but beyond an arm is ridiculous." And it was not necessary to go further. He was left with a whole frame, but a brown arm set in a permanent attitude of a man wanting to shake hands.

A few days later we watched the monthly extraction of poison. Although it was eight o'clock in the morning we were not the only sightseers at the basement room at the back of the Pasteur Institute. A score of European women and children had gathered to stare through the thick windows and wire screen as some forty Gabon vipers were treated. The snakes lay, each in its thick wooden box, scattered about the floor. The four African assistants, wearing white uniforms and thick protective goggles, went about their job under the supervision of French doctors. First one of them opened a box, reached in with a forked stick and trapped the snake round its neck. Then he would reach down with his gloved hand and grip the beast behind the head. The Gabon viper is not a pretty sight as it lashes and writhes in protest. About five feet in length, as thick as a man's calf, it has the dull green and yellow and brown markings of British vipers writ large. A snarling mongrel's head, flat and thick, adds the last word in ugliness. Sometimes, in moments of special range, it flickers a long tongue in and out.

The principal black-poison extractor, who has no chin and a suffering look like a torturer, holds the serpent out at arm's length in the center of the room. An assistant clamps its upper jaw with a pair of sharp pincers and bends the mouth wide open. A second assistant slips a saucer under the poison tooth and draws off the liquid.

When the snake has been neutralized, a third assistant stuffs raw meat down its gullet with tweezers and then pours a half pint of water in to wash down the meal. To help the snake digest they press the food along the length of its body before throwing it back into its box.

"Snakes in captivity often become lethargic," said Dr. Jean Demarchi, who has many times performed the extraction himself. "They lose their appetite and have to be forcibly fed. If you put live mice and rats into their cage they will kill them, but not eat them." He specialized in snakes. They send the venom back to the Pasteur Institute in Paris, where it is tested on horses and made into serum. "Each Gabon viper produces up to seven grams of venom a month," he explained. "The mamba, on the other hand, produces very little. But what it produces is very deadly. It is easy to catch the Gabon viper. They are found in Brazzaville itself. But we have no mambas in captivity, because we can't catch any. They are very fast, very aggressive, very deadly, and the natives have a superstitious terror of them." I suggested that this terror was not in the least superstitious but simply realistic. The scientist could not understand this argument. So far we had been speaking outside the glass separating the extraction room. They said we could not go in until snake 35 was ready for extraction. I had imagined that this must be a particularly docile creature, but I had not allowed for the scientific sense of fun. Snake 35 fought and writhed and spat until it was gagged by the hunks of raw meat. Remembering the brown plastic arm which had been won only a few months back, I stepped inadvertently backwards, only to hear a concerted hiss from the snakes in their cages behind. I understood that the French snake men, for all their pose of scientific detachment, had suffered a touch of the Congo.

In Leopoldville I had looked with longing over the gray Congo to Brazzaville. "It's a delightful place," people said, "just like a provincial French town." Certainly it has all the disadvantages. A non-French diplomat gave me this view of Brazzaville life: "What do people do? The worst thing about it is not being able to get away. After thirty miles the road stops and becomes a dirt track. Of course if you want to you can wade out into the Congo rapids with a trusted native guide. And then there's tennis and golf, but I haven't sunk as far as that yet. There are two night-clubs, the Hi-fi and the Scotch. At the Hi-fi, they say, you can come to an arrangement to get a French girl for 5,000 CFA. But the Scotch is no good unless you come with a girl. Of course, you can always get a black girl. For instance, there are two fifteen-year-old sons of some French friends of mine who have their black girl friends already. They call them 'our redheads.' It doesn't sound so bad that way. It's all very respectable and middle class, and it's not a place for bachelors. There are few white women, except for a handful of eighteen-year-olds in their last year at *lycée*, and the not-so-young marrieds who are beginning to smell of the tomb. And I must say the Frenchmen lay about both sorts with gusto. But since you're not likely to get very far with a schoolgirl it comes down to sleeping with someone else's wife . . .

There's no club. The French are not very clubbable. But on Bastille Day they hold a parade at Army H.Q. and a formal party at the Embassy. And in the Scotch Club in the evening they are all very stiff and correct with tightly buttoned lips."

There are bowls outside the cinema on a Sunday night, with the whole French community and half the bats and cockchafers in the Congo. The Africans play football, and some of the trainers are French, but the only white face in the crowd is a priest with a yellow cigarette drooping into his beard. There are outdoor cinemas where you sit on clanging metal seats, and where bats skim continually in front of the screen. The young French boys in the front of the audience kicked the seats and sniggered whenever anybody said "fesses" in the dialogue, which was often. Their African nannies, sitting directly behind, gave an indulgent titter in sympathy.

Congo-Brazzaville is the southernmost of the fourteen states formed from French Equatorial and French West Africa. Two of these, Mali and Guinea, have taken the leftward path to independence, therefore disdaining French aid and influence. The rest use a currency tied to the French franc; they sell most of their produce to France; they raise loans from the French Government and capital from French firms. The French Army is stationed in most of these countries, and even in Gabon, where it was not stationed, troops were flown in to put down a left-wing government that threatened France's supply of plutonium.

All these fourteen countries put together have a population of thirty million, or considerably less than Nigeria. More than nine tenths of the area is desert, swamp, scrub or jungle, so inhospitable that it was not explored until the end of the last century and so intractable that it remains uncultivated. With the exception of Senegal, halfway up the west coast of the continent, most of these countries have an oppressive, unhealthy climate. Consequently, and thanks also to wise policies on the part of French Government, there have been almost no *colons*, or French property owners, here.

This helps to explain the peaceful change of power. French policy in Africa was always multiracial in that educated Africans were regarded as French citizens. Many African leaders today have sat in the French Parliament and lived in France itself as lawyers, doctors or even as mayors of French towns. Until late in the 1950s the French kept up the pretense that all French Africa was actually part of France. This was easier for them to pretend because most of the French territories stretching through Algeria to the Congo formed a compact mass on the map. It was not, like the British Empire, spread out over five continents.

But the pretense could not last. No amount of rhetoric could convince Africans, inspired by the wave of nationalism sweeping the whole continent, that they were really black Frenchmen. In 1958 the newly elected President de Gaulle offered to all the French territories south of the Sahara the chance to vote themselves independent or to become self-governing republics within the French community. Only Guinea voted for independence and got it immediately, perhaps too immediately for her liking. The French cleared out almost overnight, leaving the country stripped of trained men and of materials. The remaining countries, who had voted to stay in the community, took the hint. Next year de Gaulle offered these countries full independence outside the French community but with a guarantee of continued French aid, both moral and material. All the countries took this opportunity, although Mali later broke away from federation with Senegal and followed a line of complete independence *à la* Guinea. French policy towards its former colonies has been far more clear-cut than Britain's towards hers. The French demand that their African countries stay friendly or get out altogether. The British, on the other hand, have continued to give aid to countries like Ghana, Kenya and Tanganyika, whose governments have often behaved in a way displeasing to Britain. It has also had a marked difference on the lives of the Europeans in former colonies. The British stay on to work in Ghana, Kenya, or Tanganyika, but they do so very much on the sufferance of the host government. They are threatened by harassment or even unexplained dismissal.

The eighty thousand French people in former French Africa can work and live with complete freedom from interference. They may complain of slowness or inefficiency on the part of the African host countries, but never of unwarranted interference. They have paid the piper and make damn sure he keeps playing their tune.

At least this is the cynical explanation. It may be that the French avoid friction simply because they are better at getting on with the newly independent people. I have noticed the same excellent relationship in Indochina, where the French have far less economic influence and where other Europeans, and the Americans, are most unpopular. Nor should one deduce that the British have an invariably prickly relationship with their former colonies. There is no animosity in India nor in such African countries as Nigeria and Sierra Leone.

Who are these eighty thousand Frenchmen? The overwhelming majority of them live in the two great ports and industrial cities of Abidjan, in the Ivory Coast, and Dakar, former capital of French West Africa and now capital of Senegal. The remaining French, perhaps one to four thousand in each country, are the teachers, technicians and administrators who carry on the *mission civilisatrice* to the young and often extremely poor republics. These were the types I had met in Brazzaville and was to meet again in Chad.

Fort Lamy, the capital of the Republic of Chad, lies at the desolate center of the immense continent; and it feels like it. It was the rainy season when I arrived, with a climate like hot Irish stew. The River Chari is joined here by a tributary bearing a different color of mud, so that for a few hundred yards the two streams flow side by side without merging, in three layers of red, green and white, like Neapolitan ice cream. Millions of herons and egrets, most of them brilliant white, fly to and fro, up and down the river, in a kind of unending aerial Oxford Street of traffic. There are butterflies big as both your hands and armies of lizards, colored like red-hot pokers, doing their press-ups in the public gaze. Because of the frequent rains, the town authorities have built deep cement gutters along the side of the road which serve also as homes for the bullfrogs. These animals have discovered that a single burp from the bottom of one of these gutters resounds through Fort Lamy with all the satisfactory uproar of naval gunfire. The French quarter is still colored differently on the map from the African quarter of thick, mud houses. The French have preserved their Avenue de Gaulle and a network of smaller streets named after his generals and colonels. The Chadiens are themselves very Gaullist, taking a pride in the fact that here, in Fort Lamy in 1940, the West Indian Governor of French Equatorial Africa proclaimed for the Free French, while his counterpart in French West Africa supported Vichy. The pride of the town is the still unfinished Catholic cathedral, with its cement walls and yellow and black tiled roof. There is a hollow space under the steps up to the west entrance. I looked underneath to find that a bare-breasted African woman, with children and chickens, had made this basement her home.

Chad is the scene of Romain Gary's novel *The Roots of Heaven* about Morel, who loves elephants and fights the world to protect them from slaughter. To him elephants were a symbol of liberty. In Nazi concentration camps during the war he would comfort himself with the thought of them: "When I couldn't stand it any longer, I would close my eyes and think of the herds of elephants at liberty, running freely across Africa, hundreds and hundreds of magnificent animals that nothing can resist—no cement wall, no barbed wire, nothing; they rush forward over the great open spaces and smash everything in their way, and nothing can stop them. That's liberty, I tell you."

In Romain Gary's book, and in fact, Chad was a gathering-place for the derelicts of the world: a British retired colonel, an American turncoat in the Korean war turned alcoholic, and a *demi-mondaine* from war-torn Berlin. Such people have gone now from Chad and Brazzaville, although there are still a few left in the Central African Republic. There, if you buy a hat in the shop, they will ask if you want a *chapeau brousse* (bush hat) or a *chapeau chapeau.* There are a few white deadbeats left. But in Chad, the last French "undesirable" had been deported with the complicity of the French Embassy three weeks before I arrived. "*The Roots of Heaven* was an acceptable book," said the Embassy information officer, "but the film was abominable." Chad had been shocked by the behavior of some of the moviemakers.

The typical Chad Frenchman of today can be found at the Office of Scientific and Technical Research Overseas, an organization with branches throughout French-speaking Africa. Here they are studying hydrology and marine biology to increase the fish supplies of the Chari; they also have plans to cultivate the northeast shores of

Lake Chad. Some countries here believe that Chad could become the breadbasket of Africa.

We went out in the Office boat to collect plankton in jam jars. André Iltis, the marine biologist, said that this was one of the most fish-rich rivers in the world. He liked Africa and hoped to stay on in Chad after his tour of duty. Before coming here four years ago he had served in the Army in Algeria. Yes, but that was a *different* Africa. "Here I like the climate, and there is still some adventure left. If you drive a couple of hundred miles, you don't know what's going to happen, you're completely on your own. And if anything happens to you, well, you have to sort it out for yourself. There won't be any mechanics around."

Two years ago the French Government instituted a most intelligent version of military service by which young men with special skills, such as doctors, engineers and sociologists, could do the best part of their national military service as civilians in one of the French-speaking underdeveloped countries. The graduate, for so most of them are, has to do three months of basic military training, which probably comes towards the end of his service. The remaining eighteen months are spent in the field. In Chad alone there are a score of these young men. Although it might sound like a Peace Corps by draft, it is in fact purely voluntary. I talked to Jean Courtin, a prehistorian attached to the Chad Institute of Human Studies. "We had to apply for the job in this *service civile*. They screened us to make sure, for instance, we weren't Communists. But there are a lot of people with the qualifications who don't want to apply for it because it means going to Africa. They prefer to stay in the Army with a good chance of remaining in France near their families and their girl friends."

Jean Courtin studied prehistory at Paris and then did research on the rock paintings in his native Provençe. He came out to Chad four years ago and was already in his present job when the time came for call-up. It must be one of the best assignments any man could have for national service. Every winter, when the weather cools enough, he goes by Land Rover into the desert of northeast Chad near the Sudan border, in search of rock carvings and paintings that date to 5000 B.C. The photographs reveal some very exciting discoveries. They show giraffes, noosed round the leg in a trap, trumpeting elephants and hunters with bows and arrows, all in an area that has long since surrendered to desert. Because these drawings were done on the lee side of hills, they have resisted the sandstorms and stand out in great clarity. During the summer Courtin returns to the folklore museum in Fort Lamy to work over his findings. And about once a year he leaves Chad for a holiday in his home town of St. Tropez. "But it's much calmer here," he says.

The social life of Fort Lamy is concentrated on the river. For the French there is "le club," which they pronounce with the English "u," where "le boy" will bring you "un whisky soda" as you watch the other members water skiing. Incidentally, the word "boy" does not offend the French Africans. Similarly in Nairobi, it is all right to call the waiter *garçon.* The Chadiens use the river for their ablutions and for their food. They go out in a dugout, lower a big triangular net from the stern and then bang on the hull to attract the fish. Swoosh, the net is lifted and found filled with fish. Many more sit on the bank with primitive rods and lines baited with strips of fish or animal gut. It is common to see them haul in a fish every five minutes. The average weight is a pound, and it is not hard to hook one of the giant *capitaines.* In the evening the river boils with the fish rising to seize flies and ants on the surface. Idly I caught a big ant and dropped it off the landing place into the river below. A large fish took it with such violence that I almost fell in with shock. Promptly I asked at the hotel if I could hire some fishing equipment. They shrugged. That evening I asked several Frenchmen the same thing. They looked rather puzzled and amused. No, nobody fishes here, they said. They swim and water ski in the river but do not fish. Not for the first time I was bewildered by France. At home they are zealots for fishing. Any stream in France with the reputation for trout is lined with anglers whose bamboo rods look like a fence. The fishermen for gudgeon in the Seine are the most pathetic, because the least rewarded, of any I know in the world. Yet none of these Frenchmen fishes the Chari. Dare one suggest that the French, rather more than the English, are creatures of fashion? That when water skiing, a sport of exasperating boredom, is chic, they are obliged by society to water ski, and that when nobody else goes fishing, they don't go fishing, however much they might like to?

The Grand Hotel du Niger at Niamey in the Niger Republic has an elegant air-conditioned bar. Behind the bar and above the bottles there hangs an enormous photographic mural of people skiing in the Alps. The bar in the rival hotel has model DC8s mounted as though in flight. These are two great fantasies for the white man in West Africa, as he sits at the bar staring glumly in front of him and dreaming of going home. The skiing scenes, which I have seen often in French-speaking West Africa, are a particularly cruel temptation. The truth is that most Frenchmen, on boarding that dream plane for home, return to a Europe even hotter than the Africa they left. During July and August when I was visiting these countries as many as 75 per cent of all the French community were on holiday in Europe. These months in much of West Africa are among the coolest and pleasantest of the year. The French acknowledge this, but explain that the schools dictate a holiday at this time. But since the schools are in Africa, there is no reason why they should not stagger their holidays to suit the local, rather than European, weather. Eventually one always hears the same answer: "In France we go on holiday in July and August."

In countries like Niger and Chad and the Congo it is not hard to pick out the Frenchman straight from France: he is brown. The white man who lives in these steamy parts of Africa soon grows whiter than white. Even the water skiers and sunbathers retain their pallor under the pale sun of Africa. This damp, and the pale, thin, stagnant sky help to explain the chronic ill health of these parts. "For two months of the year it's not too bad," said a friend in Congo-Brazzaville. "The other ten months I feel exhausted, even from working a tropical week of thirty-five hours. I feel more tired out after the two-minute ride to work here, or five minutes by foot, than I did going an hour and a half to work in London. I'd never think of walking as far as the shop at the bottom of the road. You can't imagine the bliss it was just getting off the plane for a stop at Tripoli in the early morning and being able to breathe clean air again. And if you get a cold or, flu or even too many hangovers in a row, you can't recover unless you can get abroad or discover a quick remedy." Malaria is not yet nearly as completely conquered as people in Europe will have you believe. Every doctor I spoke to in the malarial districts of Africa had his own pet prophylactic and an utter contempt for the rest. A French chemist in the Ivory Coast saw me swallow a tablet made by a famous British chemical company. "What are you taking that for?" he asked. "Listen, I've taken pills, and a few weeks ago I nearly died of malaria. There's no cure. You might as well try to avoid a bullet aimed at your heart." The English in Africa swallow their pills, and the French prefer theirs as suppositories—to the complete unconcern of the malarial mosquito. The malaria prophylactics do not prevent but merely suppress the disease, with the result that many people in this part of Africa are continually run-down. They are like white Kenyans in reverse: soft-spoken, slow to laugh or quarrel, smaller than life.

In the smaller countries like Niger, one sees the expatriate oddities in sharp relief. In Niamey, for instance, at a time when three quarters of all the French community were away, it must have been hard to find a fourth to play bridge. Yet in the local newsheet I found an advertisement asking for players on Thursday night at the Breton Bridge Circle. The French in Africa, just like the British, take a perverse pride in their regional differences. "How do you mean what part of France do I come from? I come from Lyons," said one reproachful woman as though such a thing should be obvious even to foreigners. The only man in sweltering Niamey whom I saw wearing a suit and tie was English. But the French themselves have their own kind of formality in the tropics. At the Army swimming pool by the side of the Niger River, four fully dressed French people spotted two friends in the pool. After waving a greeting they solemnly walked to the poolside, leaned over and all four shook hands with the two in the water.

The politicians of Guinea and Mali accuse the French of neocolonialism in the countries to which they give help. Certainly private businesses have made fortunes there. Niger, for instance, is desperately short of water to irrigate the barren northern and eastern provinces. For some years French firms of water drillers have operated under contract to the Niger Government. Then an Israeli company obtained a concession to try test drills, followed soon afterwards by a British firm. A representative of the British firm assures me that after giving in his tender to the Government he was told by the President of the Republic that his, the British, tender was one tenth that of the French charge for a similar job. Indeed, the President said that the French firm had charged more for the exploratory geological survey than the British were proposing to charge for the whole operation.

The charge of neocolonialism is aimed most often at the Ivory Coast, where the French population has doubled since independence to twenty-five thousand. About 70 per cent of the Ivory Coast's trade is with France, and it is one of the few West African countries to show a steady balance-of-payments surplus. The boom came with the development of Abidjan as a modern port in 1950, when the opening of the Vridi Canal allowed the passage of ocean-going ships. The country is rich in coffee, cocoa, pineapples, bananas and other fruit, all of which get a good guaranteed price from France. There has followed a subsidiary boom in light industry and textiles and rapid development in banking, insurance, luxury shops, engineering and building. Tall offices and apartment buildings now ring the lagoons that once earned the cliché title of sleepy.

Here, as in the rest of French Africa, there is one very solid inducement to Frenchmen. For every franc (CFA) which they earn in Africa and send to France they receive two (old) francs in France. In other words, by an exchange freak, they automatically double their salaries. Moreover, their CFA salaries are suited to the high cost of living in Africa. It is the general estimate that the French in the Ivory Coast each year salt away more money in France than the French Government gives to the Ivory Coast in financial aid. Probably 70 per cent goes back to the mother country. "They're out for one thing only—the CFA," said an Abidjan diplomat. "Everything goes towards that little villa back home. And mind you they pay for it with their comfort, because the climate here is terrible."

The last point was nicely borne out by the annual report of Cobafruit, the largest banana company in Africa. On page twelve it points out, "We emphasize that, in spite of the illness of several members of the accountancy staff, the active personnel have done their utmost to set out the records in the normal time." Unfortunately I cannot say what these records show, because when M. Roger Bonamy presented me with the document he prudently tore out all those pages which, he said, "might be useful to our competitors." Suffice it to say that in ten years Cobafruit (its three directors are called Bonamy, Bonjour and Bonnet) has more than doubled its production and profits. He was anxious to point out that in agriculture itself the Europeans were growing less important: "The Europeans here are mostly in administration or banking, but in agriculture the number diminishes all the time. The great majority of planters now are African, and the process of Africanization continues. Now only 10 per cent of my office staff are European. We have night schools for things like accountancy and typing for anyone who wants to attend." Both he and M. Bonjour were proud at having made France banana-conscious. On the wall there hung a portrait of the poetess Minou Drouet with a handwritten copy of her ode to the banana:

. . . Banane, on te respire
comme au jardin
déesse à chair d'ivoire
émergeant
de ton tutu d'or
fourré de Teddy
Ma chère . . .

It is the Cobafruit equivalent of "Unzip a banana."

The Ivory Coast is reckoned the most expensive country in the world after Venezuela. A three-bedroomed house with a small garden commands a rent of £3,000 a year. If you are having the house built you are expected to pay the first three years' rent (£9,000) in advance, in cash. Even at that price the quality is not very good. Many goods have to be shipped or flown in from France, which accounts for some of the high prices. A lunch for one of soup, an omelette and yogurt, with no drinks, is likely to cost £1 10s. Ordinary hotel rooms cost from £4 upwards, although even here, as in France, the cost of two in a bed is only a fraction more than one. The cocktail bars in the more expensive hotels may charge up to 15s. for one single whisky. Often there is no pretense at charging steep prices for imported goods only. In Brazzaville, the French-run hotel charged me 4s. 6d. for a banana. They were most gruff when I refused to pay such a price. If all French-speaking Africa is expensive, the Ivory Coast seems to express it most clearly. The new Ivoire Hotel is such a palace of plutocracy that visitors to Abidjan on ocean cruises are normally taken on tour through it by a guide with a loudspeaker. After seeing those gold-plated doors, those somber, purple-tiled hallways like the nave of a cathedral, I shall always find Mr. Hilton's hostelries rather brash.

Tropics or no tropics, the French continue to eat well, and nowhere better than at the Abidjanaise Restaurant. Its chef and proprietor, M. Roland Ravaud, is a suave, neatly mustached man with none of the haggard look one might expect in one who slaved over a stove in West Africa. "He's not underdeveloped, is he?" said his lady colleague, pointing towards M. Ravaud's paunch. "In Africa one eats well." A Poitiers man, M. Ravaud came out here ten years ago to try his luck: "I had nothing at all then. I began by buying this place from some Lebanese. It was nothing then. Just a little bar and shop where you could buy a tin of meat or a packet of cigarettes or a glass of champagne—you know what the Lebanese are. It was a bazaar really." The site was good and central; office blocks rose on all sides, and soon M. Ravaud had one of the smartest restaurants in the city. "The French here are just as gastronome as they are in France," he explained. "They like to feel at home. At Christmas, for example, when it is very hot outside, we have the traditional meal starting at one o'clock in the morning. Oysters, foie gras, turkey and chestnuts, champagne. Last Christmas we went on until eight in the morning.

"Here in the Ivory Coast one can get a lot of ingredients locally. There is beef from Bamako and Niamey, there are soles and turbots and lobsters in the sea. My speciality is *Sole Farcie à l'Abidjanaise*, but the recipe is a secret. But a lot of the meat has to be flown in. The chickens come mostly from Denmark and the turkeys from France. And because of the heat, wine is likely to turn a bit, although Burgundy keeps better than claret." Although he says that the French take no interest in local food, he has himself experimented with the dish he calls *foutue*. "It's made from rice, banana, manioc, palm oil, peanuts, beef, chicken and, when possible, monkey. Yes, I've eaten monkey and it's quite good, although a bit stringy. But *foutue* is not very popular with the customers. Sometimes I do it to order, and then I have to get an African woman to come in and make it—the men don't do any cooking. No, I haven't learned the recipe myself."

Even the smallest towns in former French Africa boast at least one restaurant offering *haute cuisine*. For instance, the third-ranking restaurant in Niamey (population 40,000) has a menu including snails, *terrine du chef*, lobster, steak tartare and several French cheeses. People often laugh at the British for eating cold-weather food in hot places. In Ghana, they say, one is still offered roast beef and Yorkshire pudding, followed by plum duff and custard. But the French, in their own way, are just as little adapted to the climate. One sweltering day in the Ivory Coast, I went for a lunch to a little restaurant on the coast about thirty miles east of Abidjan. It was a tropical scene from a chocolate box. Coconut palms swayed by the side of the lagoon. We ate outdoors under a shelter of woven bamboo to the noise of the long surf and the scent of mangoes. And what were we given to eat but hors d'œuvres followed by pork chops, fat sausages, boiled potatoes and cabbage all in the style of Alsace! It was impossible to eat more than a mouthful. Nor are the French bothered by tropical superstition about sundowners. They habitually drink wine at meals, followed by cognac. Such foreign stuff as whisky and beer is often taken at nine o'clock in the morning.

There are few towns in former French West Africa without an Indochinese restaurant, serving crab soup, *nems,* chicken with bamboo shoots and that sauce which they say is made from the fermented brains of a fish. These restaurants are frequented, and sometimes kept, by the numerous old China hands in Africa, who were swept out by the Nationalists and chose Africa as the next best thing. Most of them crave the real or imagined glories of Indochina. Once, when I mentioned to one of them I had been in Phnom Penh a few months before, he actually shook my hand a second time in admiration. "If only I could go back," he said. "But why can't you?" I asked. "The country has more Frenchmen than ever now." The old China hand did not fancy the thought. Eden would never have seemed quite so attractive to banished Adam and Eve if God had relented and asked them back again.

Eating they love, and next to eating, art. Perhaps Gauguin is to blame in that most French painters with wanderlust still head for the South Sea Islands. I was therefore interested to hear of a French artist in the Ivory Coast who ran a sculpture school for Africans at Bingerville. Maître Charles Combes—and he is fond of the title Maître—is now seventy-five and has lived in Africa since the end of the First World War. He is stooping now, and yellow in the face from malaria and the tropics. He dresses in the artistic style of Edwardian *Punch* cartoons, with floppy tie, corduroy jacket and leather waistcoat, like a character from Puccini's *Bohéme.* He constantly interrupted the conversation to make spectacular and exaggerated slapping attacks on a mosquito that was roaming around his office.

"I'm a sculptor and an artist," he said, "and I came to Africa forty-six years ago. I've never once been back to France. I didn't study art in France. I'm one of those few artists who have dispensed with this training. Before the First World War I was a medical student, and then I had to serve as a doctor in the Army. But there were several of us who did not fancy the job of cutting the arms and legs off wounded men, so we became pilots. Yes, I was a pilot, and then I came out to Africa. My first job was to get to know the black people. I loved them from the very first. I stayed in the forest for several years to study magic [*fétichisme*] and I learned to agree with the English philosopher Aldous Huxley that there are more things to believe than not to believe in magic."

It is twenty-two years since he started this sculpture school on the side of a lagoon. There have always been twenty-four pupils at a time, and the first of these are now themselves sculpture teachers. Maître Combes showed me the work in progress. It would be pleasant to say that this was original and excellent. In truth these rows of heads, with fat lips and mumbo-jumbo stares, had the stereotyped sleekness of any carvings sold to tourists anywhere in Africa. I have seen the like in chromium cocktail bars in Manchester and Hamburg—a city which incidentally has its own thriving workshop of dud Africana. "All these works are entirely original to my pupils," Maître Combes said. But all of them seem to have copied the style of their master. There was little to distinguish one head from another in spite of the fanciful titles given them. "This is the face of a magician, half of whose face is disappearing under the gaze of man," he explained of a half-blank head. "This is a magician coming out of a tree, and that one is listening to the tam-tams before returning to the dance. That one is a manioc thief."

The sculptures sell well, and there are always more than enough candidates for the school. "I have to turn many of them away," Maître Combes said, "but when a boy says 'Please take me,' I know he must be really keen and I don't refuse him." An old friend of President Houphuet Boigny, Maître Combes is proud of having taken on Ivorien citizenship. Indeed, he claims to be first citizen. But he is very much displeased with the support he gets from the French business community in Abidjan: "There's a terribly low intellectual level. The mass are simply not interested in art which, they say, does not produce money." Besides running a school of twenty-four pupils, Maître Combes has also raised a family of twenty-four adopted children. "They are my black family," he said, rumpling the head of one of the last three remaining at home.

Abidjan is the new France in Africa. The old can be found at Grand Bassam, where the French first set up a government in thc 1890s. Until shortly before the war it was actually the capital of the territory. A little seaside town east of Abidjan, it is for connoisseurs of decay. The Mairie, the Governor's Palace, the customs house and the police station are all, quite literally, falling apart. Cracks have split the sides of these fine, turn-of-the-century French buildings. Ants, termites and creepers have ravaged the stucco and woodwork. All but a few of the old French families have left, to be replaced by teachers and technicians. Last July, cruel storms lashed the little hotel on the seafront. Twelve rooms were destroyed. The dining-room was gutted and all the paintings lost.

One of the few remaining French families lives in a house that once was the British Consulate. "When your people left, they took everything with them—furniture, curtains, window frames. About all they left was the flagpole. We used to hoist the tricolor on Bastille Day, but now the cord is broken." I asked this young man, who works in his father's cement works, how he and his friends amuse themselves in Grand Bassam. The answer was prompt: "By getting a car and going into Abidjan." The official houses in front of the old harbor have now been taken over by Africans. One of these, Yokon

Miezan, said that his house, too, had once been owned by the British. I asked him what work there was in Grand Bassam, and he shrugged his shoulders: "You tell me, monsieur." The pillars were peeling in the colonnades of this once-handsome port and capital. The planks in the wharf showed gaps like missing teeth. A goat stepped warily over a rotting lorry tire, and lizards scampered about among the garbage.

In the rotting African slums of Grand Bassam there are several open-air pulpits, about nine feet in height, with spiral staircases round the outside and decorative statues of silvered or gilded saints. A friend in Abidjan had said that the first Jesuit missionaries to the Ivory Coast had used these pulpits to speak to the heathen African in the marketplaces. Curious, I called at the house of the priest next to Grand Bassam Church. Too late I remembered that this was siesta time. A group of African children had gathered to bang on the door and yell for "Reverend Père." A few minutes later the poor man came to the door looking yellow and feverish with malaria. There were patches of dark brown under his eyes. "What can I do to help?" he asked. Could he tell me about the pulpits? How long ago is it since they were used by the priests? The priest frowned: "Do you mean those pulpits down at the far end of the town? The one with the statue of a man with a trumpet?" "That's right," I said, "the statue of St. Michael it looked like." The priest frowned even more angrily. "That isn't St. Michael, and if you want any more information about those pulpits you should see a woman of the town, not a priest." Apparently the Africans had used pulpits—obviously copied from the ones they saw in the churches—as platforms for their dancing girls in the most erotic moments of an orgy. Most of the Africans in the Ivory Coast believe in Islam or juju or nothing. Few people attend the Grand Bassam Church, which is also the oldest in the Ivory Coast. But in this dead town the Europeans still go out on Sunday to picnic among the tombs of the European graveyard. Here lie hundreds of French and British and Portuguese who died for their rival empires in Africa. The weeds have cracked the monumental masonry; lizards and snakes have found their way inside the graves. There are not enough white men left in Grand Bassam to tend the cemetery; soon there may be none to bury there. The capital of the colony is dead. Long live the neocolonial capital at Abidjan!

About half the French in Africa live in Dakar, capital of Senegal, on the extreme western tip of the African bulge. It was here, indeed, that the Empire began. On the island of Goree, two miles from Dakar, one sees a whole history of the French unrolled. There is a depot for slaves where the miserable Negroes were kept in chains waiting to board ship for America. There are pretty eighteenth-century houses in russet and pink stucco where the white merchants lived when Dakar was thought unsafe. There are cannons lying neglected in the alleyways, and a flight of stone steps stretching up and out to sea into nothing. At the western tip a fort has been built into the sheer, towering rock and is topped by a pair of giant naval guns which have since been spun round and knocked out of true so that they point in a lopsided way back on to Dakar. Now there is merely a rest camp for French soldiers, where they can fish off the rocks or play tennis. A statue of Blaise Diagne, first African Mayor of Dakar (and a grafter) looks down on the main square. The parasols outside the restaurant carry advertisements for Czechoslovak airlines.

The island has long been too small for the Europeans who moved on to the Cap Vert peninsula of the mainland. Now forty thousand French live on this plateau which is higher, cooler and therefore less plagued by mosquitoes than the African *medina* beyond the Cathedral. Although a few richer Africans live on the plateau, it remains almost a French town, with wide, well-kept streets, white villas decorated with flowers, a traffic problem, scores of outdoor cafés and restaurants and too many tasteless, tall office blocks. The climate is not only better than most in Africa but better than that of France. For nine months of the year there are dry sunny days with the temperature in the seventies or eighties. Even the hot, humid summer (which the French for some reason call *l'hivernage*) was no more disagreeable than a hot August day in the South of France.

No wonder the French want to stay in this very attractive city. Thanks to the friendly attitude of President L. S. Senghor they seemed even more firmly entrenched than during the days of the Empire. There are nearly five hundred French *lycée* teachers in Senegal, but only eighteen Africans. The university, which gives French degrees, has an almost all-French staff and a predominantly French student body. The Chamber of Commerce is 90 per cent French, and the total French Embassy personnel (including families) numbers a thousand. All sporting events, except football, are French, and all films shown on the plateau are either French or dubbed. (The Africans, incidentally, prefer the Arab and Indian films shown in the *medina.*) There are two thousand French troops in the country, and Senegal's navy is officered entirely by French officers—five of them. *Hæute couture* prevails in the cocktail parties, the *Code Napoléon* in the law courts and English dirty literature in the bookshops. The Africans there have learned the old French skill of simultaneously shrugging the shoulders, raising both hands with fingers extended outwards in a sign of bewilderment, smoking a Gauloise, pouting the lower lip and driving a car. They have inherited the French love of notices telling you what not to do. I particularly liked the scrawl on the wall of a back street in Dakar: "*Défense de stationner et d'uriner.*"

As in the Ivory Coast there has been a drift of Frenchmen away from the country into the town. The economic power has shifted this way; moreover, Africans have taken over from Frenchmen as regional administrators. According to the French, there is no real economic jealousy between the races. "The only anxiety comes from the small shopkeepers," said a French economic journalist. "In lines such as shirts and socks they used to be sole agents for various European brands. Now that the Senegalese are manufacturing clothes, anyone can deal in any brand. Also the shopkeepers suffer from the fact that the new class of French technical assistants, who are the bulk of the French community, don't spend very much. The old colonialist would spend every penny he earned right here in Dakar. These new ones may go to the cinema once a week, but otherwise they buy everything during their four months a year in France. They send presents back home at Christmas, but you can bet they bought the presents during the summer in France. The only thing they buy here is the string to wrap the parcels. The typical French teacher here, a little Socialist in a tropical shirt with his wife going out to work, spends only a fraction of what he earns."

How much do they earn? A newly arrived junior executive gets about CFA 80,000-100,000 a month (£1= CFA 650) and a manager about CFA 200,000 a month. This comes to about £3,700 a year. If he saves £1,000 of this and sends it back to France, where its value is automatically doubled, he can easily save £2,000 a year. A man who saves more than he spends can therefore actually save more than he earns. Most companies and the Government provide their employees with accommodations, car and regular free flights for them and family back to France. And of course here, as everywhere among whites in Africa, the wives generally go out to work as well. "Many young couples," the journalist went on, "for example, when the man is a works manager or a foreman, save everything he earns and live on her salary. These are people who live fairly cheaply and without a servant." The barmaid at my hotel was just such a young wife. Her husband works as a salesman from eight to five. She works as a barmaid from noon until midnight. "He's always asleep by the time I get home," she explained, but added with true *oo-la-la* roguishness, "I always wake him up, of course, and don't let him go back to sleep until two o'clock in the morning."

In Chad, Niger and Congo-Brazzaville, when I asked French people why they had come out to Africa, they would sometimes say "for the adventure." In Abidjan or Dakar there is really no such inducement. "Most people come here by chance," said the journalist. "They saw an advertisement in the newspaper or their firm has a branch here. They just think that Dakar or Abidjan sounds more interesting than Lyons or Bordeaux. Those who come out by chance are quite uninterested in politics or social questions. They have no prejudices either way. Among the technical assistants, on the other hand, there is a type of idealist who wants to solve the problem of Africa. And even when you point out to him that the problem has existed a very long time, he merely replies that in all that time nobody knew the solution." Either this type is very rare or he must have been on holiday. Not one of the many French people I met gave any altruistic motive for coming to Africa, and I hasten to add that I find this admirable. The kind of person who arrives with feelings of generalized altruism is quick to turn bitter as soon as his goodwill is slighted. The Africans do not need sympathy. They need more money and more efficiency. The Europeans who value these two things for themselves are often the kind who pass them on to Africa.

If there was any racial tension anywhere in West Africa, one might expect to find it in Dakar. It is the only part where the whites are numerous enough to be a minority rather than just a colony. Indeed, during the recent war when the Vichy Government introduced certain color bars, there was considerable animosity between the plateau and the *medina.* There is almost no trace of this left. A Frenchman who has lived here since the war says, "Even the left-wing opposition Africans do not raise the subject. They're perfectly friendly with me, although I'm no revolutionary. If there is a cause of difficulty it's the educational backwardness of those Africans who have had a primary education but nothing more. It's difficult to get on with them, but for educational rather than racial reasons. I would say that seven times out of ten when a Frenchman in Dakar is holding some kind of social gathering there will be Africans among his guests. And this is entirely without *arrière-pensée.* There is paternalism, but it exists only towards servants. There are scarcely any racists or fanatics here. The Algerian *pied noir* didn't come down here. Most of them went to France or to North America. But both the French and the Africans do have a certain racial prejudice against the Syrians and the Lebanese. You will very seldom find any of them at a party, however rich they are.

"There is an interesting change in the pattern of intermarriage here in Senegal. Before the war children of mixed marriages generally had a white father and a black mother. Now it's the other way round. It's quite common for a black boy to marry a white girl. This is because it's mostly the boys who go to study in France. Many of them get married. Here they couldn't marry a white girl. There are very few single women here, and it's very rare for a white man to marry a white girl. Nor is it common here now for a white man to have a black girlfriend. They are more racist than the women and they think it a sign of admission of failure to go out with one." Not once in any French-speaking country in Africa did I meet or see a Frenchman with an African wife.

An Asian diplomat in Dakar morosely prophesied that the troubles of South Africa would soon affect the whole of the continent and that the black Africans would turn against the whites and Asians, even in distant Senegal. So far there is no sign of it. The West Africans trade with South Africa and not even the Left protests. During the troubles in Brazzaville early this year an angry crowd roaming the streets turned its very unfriendly attention on a lone European. "Where are you from?" they asked, no doubt imagining he was a Frenchman or American. The man very bravely replied, "I'm a South African." To his surprise the crowd clustered round to shake his hand and slap him on the back. As an African, he was one of them.

There is enough racial hatred in the world without reading it into countries where it does not exist. European logic may deduce that because the whites in South

Africa ill-treat the blacks, the blacks in West Africa will ill-treat the whites. This is not African logic. It would not be rash to say that there is far less anguish about race—with all the concomitant boredom and hysteria—in West Africa than in West London. It is not a subject that worries the French. The African intellectuals talk much about concepts of "negritude," but this has never been turned to animosity against the whites.

The tiny British colony of Gambia, which became independent in February 1965, is a fascinating contrast to surrounding Senegal—and a captivating country.

Customs, Immigration and Health at Yundum Airport each gave me a splitting smile and a "Welcome to Gambia." Seeing the word "journalist" on my passport, they promptly began an informative if hilarious forum of argument on West African politics. There was a technical fault that delayed the plane on its way on to Freetown, with the result that all the passengers were tucking into free drinks at the expense of Nigerian Airways. A great many local Gambians seemed to have turned up for a drink as well, even at nine o'clock in the morning, because, as they all say, it is the best bar in town. The English lady behind the bar was discussing her home county of Westmorland with a Nigerian: "Just to hear you talk about Kendal makes me excited." Everyone in the airport, whether white, brown or black, seemed possessed by laughter and friendliness. "Is it always like this?" I asked an Englishman. "Yes, always," he said, "this place is as near as possible to an earthly paradise, and I just pray that independence doesn't spoil it."

Gambia was the first British colony in Africa and very nearly the last. A tiny splinter of land on the banks of the Gambia River, it was always a difficult country to find on the map and now, what with Zambia, it will be harder still. The population of 320, 000 is enclosed on all sides by Senegal, and one of the main topics of Gambian politics was whether to join with the French-speaking country in some kind of association. The Senegalese were not very concerned about it. "They don't give a damn whether Gambia joins them or not," I was told in Dakar. Nor are the problems of Gambia of much interest to the unfortunate many who have not been there. But the juxtaposition of former British and former French countries does provide an intriguing study in European cultural influence.

The remaining British in Gambia—less than a hundred of them—cannot look with much pride on what they have done for the colony during 376 years of rule. The capital, Bathurst, is a sad contrast to Dakar. Here goats scavenge the shabby streets, which are named after Wellington and his generals. The houses are mostly of corrugated iron or of tin. There is not one bookshop except for a Methodist mission that sells tracts. Although the soil is fertile, the Gambia River full of fish and the climate mild, the colony is poor. Groundnuts are almost the only produce, and the average income of a farmer is about £22 a year. A few Indians and Mauritanians run bazaars, but most of the wealth of the colony is controlled by Levantine merchants and by the United Africa Company. And for clever merchants, Gambia is a most lucrative territory. The surrounding Republic of Senegal has punitive tariffs on incoming goods and therefore very high prices. Gambia has a liberal trade policy. Therefore, since Senegalese customs men are easily bribed, a great part of Gambia's legal imports are re-exported by smuggling into Senegal and even as far as Mali and Guinea. If one believed that all goods shipped to Bathurst went for legitimate home consumption, then every Gambian man, woman and child must buy one pair of shoes and one bottle of whisky a week. Some of the Syrian and Lebanese merchants have grown very rich, and at the Cedars Club, where they gather, thousands of pounds often change hands in an evening through gambling. But very little of Gambia's profits return to the Gambians. The British excuse themselves by saying that Gambians can't work, or won't. In fact, those who have got training and jobs prove excellent workers. Those who have not often migrate to Dakar. Even more than most Africans, the Gambians have a passion for study. You frequently see them poring over a textbook during a pause in their work; sometimes they stay out late at night in the streets in order to read under the light of a street lamp.

An Englishman who is far from liberal in his views said of the Gambians, "What never fails to amaze me about these people is that they're so bloody nice. Considering how little we've done for them I wouldn't be surprised if they cut our throats." He exaggerates British ineptitude, of course. In terms of grants, scholarships and good administration, the British colonial Government has put more into Gambia than it has taken out. Its failure has been in not promoting economic activity that would benefit the Gambians rather than foreign or British businessmen. But my friend did not exaggerate the niceness of the Gambian and the excellent racial relationships in the country.

Everywhere I met the same smiles and hospitality as at Yundum Airport. The white motorist, who in Kenya can expect scowls or even stones, is greeted everywhere with waves and shouts. If the villagers know your name they actually chant a greeting as you go by. Even dowdy Bathurst seems gay by virtue of its citizens. The Gambian girls, in Lumumba blouses and gaudy Arab turbans, are the liveliest and the loveliest in all Africa. The Bathurst working man sets off his patched trousers and shirt by sporting a yellow, plastic trilby, made in Japan. Even the souvenir peddlers—those intercontinental pests—are acceptable here in Bathurst. One of them nudged my elbow as I sat at the bar of the Atlantic Hotel. "Very nice wallet. Only one pound." "No, thanks!" I said without looking round. "All right, ten shillings," he said—and then "eight shillings." He was so patient and courteous that I felt embarrassed and bought one of his wallets for ten shillings, whereupon he sat down at the next bar stool, ordered himself a bottle of tonic water and chatted to me for half an hour about life, his family and the political situation.

The price of drinks is a very important factor in racial relationships. Cafés and bars are the natural meeting-places for whites and blacks alike, and in all independent countries they are open to everyone. But where drink is very expensive few Africans can afford imported beers and spirits. In Southern Rhodesia drink is cheap enough, but whites and blacks keep to their separate bars. In Gambia, as in the rest of British-speaking West Africa, mixing is considered perfectly natural.

The remnants of the British colonial colony still retain their own club in the fashionable suburb. "You won't see many Africans there," said one Englishman, "unless they're married to one of the members. I've been excluded by them just because I had a bloody black girl-friend." The Lebanese Cedars Club is also patronized by the French and a few English people. The best one in town is the Bathurst Reform Club, which is a meeting place for the African intelligentsia. I was kindly invited there by S. B. Hartie—it is always initials rather than Christian names in Gambia—and discovered a big, blue-walled room like a British Legion Club, with a dart-board in the corner and a billiards table under the slowly whirring fans. The members and guests, who included a handful of Europeans, were enjoying an evening of beer, cards and politics. And, of course, bingo. I could scarcely hear the politics for the game: "We used to send our officers to Sandhurst . . . Doctor's orders—Number nine . . . Now, of course, we send them to Senegal . . . twenty-one—key of the door . . . It's the trade unions who are behind this." The main excitement came when a Nigerian won two games running and when for ten minutes the Assistant Commissioner of Police chased and killed a bat with his walking stick.

Gambia is more English than England, more English even than India. They are cricket mad, needless to say, and play an annual test match against Sierra Leone. They are also pools mad. Each of the big companies has an office in Bathurst where the Gambians place their weekly shilling or half-crown. At Littlewoods alone they take £200 a month, although, as a Gambian told me pathetically, "It's very difficult for us out here, as we don't know anything about the teams." In one Bathurst hotel there is piped music playing selections, so it seemed to me, of the theme tunes from second-rate British war pictures. There was also tinned soup and difficulty in getting drinks except during limited hours. But the absolute Englishness of Gambia was revealed in the transit lounge of Dakar Airport on the way home. A young Gambian, who is a pilot in the R.A.F., was airing his views on Senegal: "Terrible lot of flies here. You won't find that in Gambia. It's the cleanest country in Africa. And look at that Senegalese policeman. Trousers too short. Pockets not pouched. I'd have him in the guardroom in no time."

Less than a hundred Englishmen in Gambia divide into those who mix almost exclusively with the other English, and those who mix with white and black alike. The more exclusive were found among the Colonial Office officials and merchants. The doctors and schoolteachers fell in the second group. Those who mixed most easily of all were the old African hands. For instance,

Davey Jones, an Irish engineer, and the first white man on the committee of the Bathurst Reform Club, came to Gambia after eighteen years in Africa, including South Africa. His friend Geoffrey Morton, who is hoping to open up tourism and a cotton industry in Gambia, was twenty-six years in Kenya.

The manner of Morton's arrival in Gambia is typical of the old Africa hands. He has had a varied career: in printing, the textile industry, as an officer in the Special Branch during Mau Mau and briefly as one of Tshombe's white soldiers in the Congo trouble. With his bull neck, Vandyke beard and booming laugh, he reminds one of certain old sailors. Indeed, only a few months before he had been preparing to sail his own boat to the Seychelles Islands to settle there. By chance he had met the Gambian High Commissioner at a cocktail party, and within weeks he and his two business partners were persuaded to switch their investment from the Seychelles to Gambia.

Once I asked Mr. Morton why he preferred the Reform Club to the Bathurst. "I never go there. That's where the English go," he explained, as though this was self-evident. Normally he refers to them as the expatriates. He thinks of himself not as an Englishman but as an African. But, as so often happens, Morton and Jones and the fellow whites in Gambia who are quite multiracial in outlook are not in the least liberal in their views. "Some of the expatriates here call me a bolshie," Morton told me, "but there's nobody more conservative than me." He and Davey Jones condone the régime in South Africa, yet they like and respect the Gambians. It is a paradox that bewilders and therefore shocks liberal Europeans; when you begin to understand it, you begin to understand the white man in Africa.

As with many Englishmen, my idea of the west coast of Africa had been based on Graham Greene's *The Heart of the Matter*. I reread it on the journey with somewhat less respect than before. He piles on the horrors a bit too thick. Vultures play round the house like sparrows; when Scobie goes for a wash there is a rat perched on the side of the bath: " 'Why,' he wondered, swerving the car to avoid a dead pye-dog, 'do I love this place so much? Is it because here human nature hasn't had time to disguise itself? Nobody here could ever talk about a heaven on earth.' " This is clearly why Graham Greene loved the place, and all other places that whiff of corruption. Typically he took a steamer trip up the Congo to get material for *A Burnt Out Case*, which the French translate as *La Saison des Pluies*. A journalist covering the recent troubles of Haiti under its voodoo-fascist régime was to remark that almost the only other guest in the hotel was Graham Greene.

After visiting Senegal and Gambia I began to wonder whether, in fact, Greene did not exaggerate the horrors of West Africa. The climate was quite agreeable, even during the hot rainy season. Most of those who complained of "low coast fever" could equally well be suffering from a hangover or boredom. There were plenty of birds to look at besides vultures. Perhaps, I thought to myself, Greene would not have reacted in quite so depressed a fashion if he had lived in Gambia or Senegal rather than Freetown. Then I chanced on one of his travel books from before the war and found that Greene had indeed passed by this part of the coast on his travels. He did not like it:

"In the restaurant, a little drunk on iced Sauterne, one didn't trouble about the Dakar one had heard about, the Dakar of endemic plague and an unwieldy bureaucracy town on the coast . . . Undoubtedly the other Dakar (the Dakar of the 416 dead, of the despair and injustice) was there, but something else was momentarily shining through, something which was always stubbornly existing." A little way down the coast he saw "the hawks flapping heavily over Bathurst, a long, low backcloth of houses and trees along a sandy beach; a swarm of figures in the native quarter like flies on a piece of meat; the not being allowed to land because of yellow fever; the sense of isolation that the woman had as she went off to join her husband in the quarantined town." *

Mr. Greene was never one to look at the world through rose-tinted spectacles, but even so there is something grotesque about this description. The imagery of the flies on the meat gives him away. So might Graham Greene describe a cluster of angels in paradise.

* *Journey Without Maps* (Heinemann).

Epilogue

SOME FIFTY YEARS ago there was a tedious story about a clubman who said, "At the beginning of every year, I prophesy trouble in the Balkans. And, dammit, I'm always right." Now, of course, he would always be wrong, because the Balkans have become one of the most placid areas of the world. Africa has taken over the world headlines. The palace revolts, assassinations and clan wars of Serbia, Bulgaria and Greece have now been transferred to Ghana, Tanganyika and Zanzibar. Names like Nish, Scutari and Sofia are out of the world's editorials. Names like Usumburu, Zomba and Bamako are in. The Congo, not Macedonia, is a synonym for political chaos. Therefore, in theory, the only worthwhile prophecy to be made about Africa is of chaos, and it is idle to speculate on the fate of the whites. They themselves are inclined to be apprehensive. "If you're writing about the white man in Africa, you've come only just in time," was a comment heard more than once. I believe that much of this pessimism is groundless.

The white rulers in Africa should be able to hold on

for a few decades. The white armies of South Africa, Southern Rhodesia, Angola and Mozambique are more than a match for their black African opponents. Perhaps the Algerians are a threat, but a distant one. The Nigerians and the Ethiopians have good armies, but do not seem inclined to be militant. The Nationalists in Angola and Mozambique may grow strong enough to oust the Portuguese through terrorism, but so far their efforts have only served to consolidate Portuguese rule by making it more efficient. The war in Angola has meant a greatly increased white population and a network of strategic roads and airfields where none existed before. The best hope for independence in Portuguese Africa lies in an overthrow of the Government in Lisbon. The liberal opposition would certainly set the African "provinces" on the way to independence. As for South Africa, I can see no chance of overthrow from within for at least the next twenty years. Time may have overtaken any comments on Southern Rhodesia; but whatever occurs in that sullen land, I am heartily glad not to be there to witness it.

If one opposes white domination in Africa—and I do—there is no reason to scoff at the role of the white men in independent countries. Far from it. Until the blacks have made huge advances in education, industry and administration, the whites are very valuable, although not perhaps indispensable. Take the case of teachers, for instance. Even in the most advanced independent countries like Ghana, Nigeria and the Ivory Coast there is a chronic shortage of teachers at primary and secondary school level. In poorer countries, like Tanganyika, classes are often taken by African teachers whose own educational level goes barely beyond reading and writing. This is not white propaganda but plain fact, acknowledged by African leaders. It may be that the former colonial powers were responsible for the lack of trained personnel. It may be that these countries were given independence too early. That is a subject beyond my ken. The fact is that any trained white teacher running a school in the bush is worth ten semieducated Africans.

The Europeans will be necessary until Africans in sufficient numbers learn technical and administrative skills. For instance, most pilots and air crews in Africa are whites. So are many engineers, architects, economists and agrarians. Senior Army officers and policemen have often been retained from the former colonial power, in spite of keen political opposition from extremists. There are even a large number of white South Africans in the armies and police forces of black African countries pledged to the overthrow of South Africa.

The whites have an even more important role in commerce and industry. At the risk of a rash generalization, I should say that the Africans have a poor instinct for business. Trading has traditionally been in the hands of Indians, Greeks, Portuguese, Levantines and Arabs. Only the Senegalese, who are partially Arab, have proved skillful at buying and selling. It would be wrong to attribute this to some racial characteristic. A commercial instinct may take centuries to develop and certainly depends on society rather than race. But ignoring the whys and wherefores, the blacks simply have not proved good businessmen—except possibly in the older industrial society of South Africa.

For this reason the key industries are still largely controlled by whites: copper in the Congo and Zambia, tourism in Kenya, bananas and coffee in the Ivory Coast, peanuts in Senegal, diamonds in Tanganyika. Again, this is not a proof, as the racists argue, of white superiority. It means only that jobs like running a mine, cannot be learned from books by however brilliant a student. They come from a tradition of skill. The Belgians of the Union Minière are often mining men from the coalfields of Europe who have transplanted themselves to the tropics. Doc Williamson, who struck diamonds in the Tanganyikan bush, was a Canadian, trained in South Africa, with the flair of the born prospector. Those African countries which hope to attract thousands of tourists from Europe will need plenty of Swiss to run their hotels for them.

One could even argue, at the extreme risk of racial boasting, that Europeans have a particular restless enterprise which has so far been lacking in Africans. It was Europeans like Park, Stanley and Livingstone who opened up Africa. It was Europeans like the Voortrekkers, Rhodes and de Brazza, who conquered it. These explorations and conquests may not have been admirable, but they attest to a kind of aggressive determination which helps to build nations. Of course, this quality has its bad side. The enterprise of the Europeans goes with belligerence and savagery. The modern Africans are peaceful folk by comparison. People who talk of the Balkanization of Africa should remember this: there are no signs of the Balkan wars between these tiny states. In the chapter on Portuguese Africa I mentioned that comical statue in Lourenço Marques showing a white mother—Europe—protecting the black boy—Africa. It would be truer to change the sexes. Africa is passive, calm, feminine. Europe is restless, aggressive—sowing the seeds both of order and anarchy. The whites have brought slave-trading, religious intolerance, racism, alcoholism, Communism, napalm bombs and industrial slums. They have also brought justice, hospitals, literacy, D.D.T., liberalism and industrial wealth. They have dispersed the tribes and reformed them. They have slaughtered wild game and preserved it. They have enslaved the black man, and made his brother a graduate of Cambridge.

The English in independent Africa have a difficult time ahead of them. Even since I visited Kenya several whites have been expelled. Some of these were evidently officials who had enemies in the Cabinet, although Jomo Kenyatta himself was thought to be hostile to the expulsions. The price of a white farm remains low, and confidence has grown shakier. Few European settlers would really be surprised if the Government wanted to buy them out for the resettlement of Africans—although naturally they would be saddened. If this should happen, the British Government should give full compensation. The settlers have a moral as well as a legal right to fair treatment in return for having behaved with such restraint since *uhuru*. Even if these farms were taken, there would still be many British in Kenya. They are active in commerce and industry, tourism and hunting, the Civil Service and education. Even if the White Highlands were turned into black co-operative farms, it would not surprise me to hear that Lord X or Air Vice-Marshal Y had stayed on his former property in the role of political commissar or State director of cattle. One should not underestimate the adaptability of the British upper classes.

The situation in Tanganyika grows more uncertain. The white community was appalled when a white man was sentenced to twenty-four lashes on a charge of fraud. The brutality of the sentence was made worse by the prisoner's history of mental disturbance. It is all very well to argue, from England, that the color of a man's skin should not affect his punishment. But the punishment is barbaric for anybody of any color. In the present surly atmosphere of Tanganyika, the whites have grounds for fear that black racial prejudice may have affected justice. Once again it can be argued that the black man in Great Britain is faced with prejudice from the police. Unfortunately this is sometimes true. But one black does not make a white. What is wrong in Britain may equally well be wrong in Tanganyika. The kind of Englishman who is inspired to work in Tanganyika by sympathy for the Africans is likely to be dismayed when a colleague gets flogged for a discrepancy in his accounts.

The French, as we have seen, manage things differently in their former colonies. No Frenchman in Niger or Chad would ever be flogged for fraud. He would scarcely be expelled from the country except at the express request of the French Embassy. It is easy to talk of these régimes as neocolonial; certainly they are financed from metropolitan France. On the other hand, the French have so far managed to maintain influence without pricking the political sensitivities of the African. Where the Africans have insisted on policies unfavorable to France, the French have either withdrawn completely —as in Guinea and Mali—or frankly intervened by force as in Gabon. Most of these former French colonies literally live off France. Except for the Ivory Coast, which has excellent natural resources, they all have a chronic trade deficit, which is met by French subsidies. The African intelligentsia, who are the natural political leaders, know that they personally could not enjoy their houses, cars and air conditioning if it were not for French aid. Life in Guinea and Mali is austere by comparison. Socialists argue that French subsidies, in return for indirect political control, can only stultify and corrupt new Africa. They argue that the go-it-alone policies of Mali and Guinea offer hope for the future, whatever the present cost in hunger and totalitarian politics.

This is the clear difference between French and British attitudes to their former colonies. The British may prefer régimes—like Sierra Leone and Nigeria—which are conservative in political and economic attitude. But Britain still offers assistance to countries like Kenya, Tanganyika and Ghana, which are socialistic, nationalist and often anti-British. When Kenya last year expelled four British subjects several London newspapers demanded the stopping of British aid until the impertinent young country was taught to behave. One writer compared British softness to the toughness of General de Gaulle. Certainly the British policy involves much swallowing of white pride, but I suspect it to be the correct one.

It is my hunch, and not much more, that the position of the whites in independent Africa will grow better rather than worse in the years to come. In Asia after the Second World War it was predicted that independence for India and Indochina would mean the expulsion of all the British and French. Today there are more British in India and Pakistan than there were before 1947. There are just as many French in Indochina; and, moreover, they are popular with the locals. Many planters still live in the parts of South Vietnam held by the Communists.

The reactionary whites say, "Of course! These people now wish they were back in the Empire." This is not true at all. I have never once, in any former colonial country, heard anyone, however sycophantic, yearn for the days of foreign rule. Independence is irrevocable. But the passing of time can, and should, mellow old hatred of the white ruler. In Cambodia, for example, the Khmers get on famously with the French, although they detest the Anglo-Saxons. Any Englishman who has recently visited India will have noticed and felt touched by the widespread and almost sentimental affection for Britain. I have attended parties in Bombay and Madras where Indian friends almost wept into their bootleg whisky as we took an imaginary walk through Bloomsbury streets and into Bloomsbury pubs. The same kind of people, often the same people, would have denounced me twenty years ago as an imperialist stooge.

We must hope that the same thing happens in Africa. There is less danger there than in Asia of Communism's sweeping away both the whites and the liberal-minded leaders. The Russians have failed miserably in their efforts to cause revolts in countries like Guinea and Ghana. The academic theories of Karl Marx have little relevance to modern industrial Europe; they have less still to agricultural, tribal Africa. The Chinese are much more of a danger. They have ignored Marxism and concentrated on stirring up the dregs of primeval savagery. They have set tribe against tribe, and encouraged the witch doctors of the world to unite. They may believe that Communism will follow chaos, but in fact only chaos will follow chaos.

The real threat to the white man's position in free Africa comes from the white man's position in slave Africa. The poison of apartheid may spread from the foot of the continent to the whole body. I have already mentioned that this argument does not seem to apply in

West Africa. Trouble in Johannesburg might spark off antiwhite riots in Dar es Salaam or Nairobi, where racial relations are anyway fairly tense. But in cities like Abidjan, Lagos or even Accra, there is little antiwhite feeling. There could be tribal battles—there often are. However, the African does not, mercifully, seem to have learned our European capacity for racial hatred on ideological grounds.

I believe in Africa for the Africans, what else? But there is room enough in this underpopulated continent for a few million white men as well. Long after Africa has been freed from white rule it will remain as part of the white man's imagination. Wild, immense, ungovernable and terrifying, it remains apart from our world. Technology cannot tame it; suburbia cannot defile it. No wonder some people feel their scalp prickle just at the sound of its name. The idea of Africa has entered into our culture. At worst is the comic white hunter, all stiff upper lip as he faces the wounded rhinos. At best are the novels of Conrad, Greene, Gary and Hemingway, who deliberately went to Africa for the truth about themselves. To the white people who live there the idea of Africa is an obsessional thrill and stimulus. Down-to-earth Kenyan farmers, Johannesburg Jewish intellectuals and hard-working Leopoldville bankers may all lapse into mystical rhetoric about Africa. The symbol of African mysticism is the elephant crossing a great plain; its effect, too often, is elephantiasis of the imagination.

Africa used to be known as the white man's grave; one

might also think of it as his cradle. People always talk of their travels in Africa as a journey back—to the interior, or the past, or the heart of the darkness. They feel that back there, somehow, there is the truth about the beginnings of life. Even the white man yearns for his Black Mother.

Index

Index